Advance Praise for *Work Optional*

"Hester's story is relatable, refreshing, and a pleasure to read. All too often we chase external measures of success without thinking about what we truly want from life. In *Work Optional*, Hester gives us a road map for a less-traveled path: living a more purpose-driven life through financial independence."

—Kristin Wong, author of *Get Money: Live the Life You Want, Not Just the Life You Can Afford*

"Tanja Hester and her partner achieved early financial independence, and in these pages she takes you on her journey. Learn why so many are firing their bosses and searching for meaning and purpose beyond cubicles and 24/7 jobs."

—Vicki Robin, *New York Times* bestselling coauthor of *Your Money or Your Life*

"This isn't just a book about how to retire early. It's a book that proves it's possible to be mindful with your spending and create a life that aligns with your values and passions—and that work can play whatever role you want it to."

—Cait Flanders, bestselling author of *The Year of Less*

"Inspirational, grounded, and thought-provoking, *Work Optional* cracks open preconceived ideas of what it means to work and what it means to live a fulfilling, purpose-driven life. Go on this adventure to learn not only the practical steps of early retirement, but more importantly, to discern what you truly want out of life. With Hester as your guide...you just might find yourself living a life you never imagined possible."

—Elizabeth Willard Thames, author of *Meet the Frugalwoods: Achieving Financial Independence Through Simple Living*

"Hester is equal parts analytical and encouraging in *Work Optional*, which helps the reader tear down any misconceptions about what it means to create a life on your terms. This will undoubtedly be a defining handbook for those looking to diverge from society's expectations of a traditional career path."

—**Erin Lowry, author of *Broke Millennial Takes on Investing***

"*Work Optional* outlines a realistic yet awe-inspiring path to a life where work is optional. There are plenty of books out there about how to save money and build wealth, but if you want to weave financial excellence into a life full of adventure, contribution, and meaning—this is the book for you."

—**Chad Carson, author of *Retire Early with Real Estate: How Smart Investing Can Help You Escape the 9-5 Grind and Do More of What Matters***

"Financial independence and early retirement are truly the ultimate life hacks, and in the page-turning book *Work Optional*, Tanja Hester lays out a concrete path to both define your future and also help you get there. This newfound freedom gives you the space to focus on what you want out of life: your projects, passions, community, and, ultimately, happiness."

—**Brad Barrett, cohost of the *ChooseFI* podcast**

"Financially independent with a bulletproof plan, Tanja gets to the heart of what actually matters in moving forward on your financial journey in *Work Optional* without resorting to the extremes sometimes found in other books on the subject. This well-researched book gives you a definitive action plan for creating a life-changing financial position in a two-phased retirement plan that is both realistic and motivating. Tips and tactics abound—one area that stuck out to me in particular was her discussion about healthcare options for those seeking early retirement—a huge area overlooked by many many seeking to make work optional or pursue nontraditional work."

—**Scott Trench, author of *Set for Life: Dominate Life, Money, and the American Dream***

WORK
OPTIONAL

Retire Early the
Non-Penny-Pinching Way

TANJA HESTER

hachette
BOOKS

New York • Boston

Hachette Books
Hachette Book Group
1290 Avenue of the Americas
New York, NY 10104
hachettebookgroup.com
twitter.com/hachettebooks

First Edition: February 2019

Hachette Books is a division of Hachette Book Group, Inc.
The Hachette Books name and logo are trademarks of Hachette Book Group, Inc.

The publisher is not responsible for websites (or their content) that are not owned by the publisher.

The Hachette Speakers Bureau provides a wide range of authors for speaking events. To find out more, go to www.hachettespeakersbureau.com or call (866) 376-6591.

LCCN: 2018960527
ISBNs: 978-0-316-45089-8 (trade paperback), 978-0-316-45087-4 (ebook)

Printed in the United States of America

LSC-C

10 9 8 7 6 5 4 3 2 1

Note to Readers

This book is presented solely for educational and entertainment purposes. The author and publisher are not offering it as legal, financial, accounting, health, or other professional services advice. While best efforts have been used in preparing this book, the author and publisher make no representations or warranties of any kind and assume no liabilities of any kind with respect to the accuracy or completeness of the contents. Neither the author nor the publisher shall be held liable or responsible to any person or entity with respect to any loss or incidental or consequential damages caused, or alleged to have been caused, directly or indirectly, by the information contained herein. No warranty may be created or extended by sales representatives or written sales materials. Every person's situation is different and the advice and strategies contained herein may not be suitable for your situation. You should seek the services of a licensed tax professional, certified financial planner, or tax attorney for counsel on your situation. As with all investments, past performance is no guarantee of future results. Please consult your physician before beginning a new diet or exercise regimen.

Contents

PART III
Thriving In Your Work-Optional Life

What you can become is the miracle you were born to be through the work that you do.

—KURT VONNEGUT

But what that work is, and how much of it you do, is up to you.

—TANJA HESTER

Introduction

It's eight p.m. on a Friday, and I'm asleep on the couch. Again. My husband, Mark, is asleep beside me. *Again.* This has become our pattern: work too much and sleep too little all week, and then collapse into the weekend, too exhausted to get through even a single 30-minute TV show. Around one a.m. I'll wake up, wake up Mark, and then trudge off to bed, and somewhere in those few dozen steps, I'll wonder, *Is this really what I've worked so hard for? Is this what success feels like?*

Work today is a far cry from work of the not-so-distant past. In the seemingly endless race to boost productivity and profits, companies expect their employees to work more and more hours for less and less pay, and to be connected even when we're not working. Entrepreneurs and freelancers are told they need to "hustle" around the clock to be successful. Sometimes it all feels just as pointless as collecting virtual coins in a video game as we chase new jobs, promotions, or opportunities that may or may not actually help us get ahead or make us happier, all the while drowning in never-ending email loops and power dynamics. We work for that paycheck, live for the weekend, and spend our money trying to soothe the stress of it all.

But you don't have to live your life according to this script just because it's what most people do. You can write your own script, one that puts you in control of your time every day—from how much work you do all the way down to whether you ever set an alarm clock again. I'll show you just how doable it is to create your own work-optional life.

I had a dream career filled with purpose, working as a communications consultant to political campaigns and nonprofits I believed in, and seeing my work directly impact people for the better. I had the privilege of working with incredibly smart, driven, and kind people, and that made the work fun much of the time. But even a great job and steady string of promotions couldn't offset the stress and exhaustion I felt constantly or help shake the feeling that I wasn't really in control of my life.

Though I loved a lot about my work, I also flew nearly a million miles during that career, spent hundreds of nights in hotels away from home, and banked more 70-hour weeks and all-nighters than I can count. The impact from my work might have felt good, but the pace of it wasn't sustainable, and I knew it. I also knew that I wasn't getting happier with each promotion. If anything, the added responsibility was making me more stressed and tired, more disconnected from the purpose behind my work, and less sure of the direction my life was taking. The higher up the ladder I climbed, the less time I had to spend with the people I care about and on the activities I love most. This put my career goals in direct opposition with the happiness and fulfillment I craved. And even when I enjoyed the work, I was still spending my time and energy on someone else's agenda, not my own.

Maybe you've had similar thoughts. You've wondered what all that time you spend working really adds up to. Or how you'll ever be able to find time in your life for the people and things that are truly important to you. You've worried that your life is passing you by, and that you might get to the end of it and realize you didn't do what you'd always dreamed of doing or what would give your life meaning. Maybe you've chased money or prestige, but realized that getting it didn't make you any happier, and you only had to work more year after year to hang on to your position.

It was during all that ladder climbing and questioning that I met my husband, Mark, who was also on a steep trajectory in an equally demanding career as a political researcher. We were proud of our careers and felt incredibly fortunate to work for companies and people we respected, but we saw the toll those careers were taking: how little we were sleeping, how much the stress was impacting our health, how unable we were to disconnect for more than an hour or two, how desperately we came to need the weekends (even if we often worked or slept through them) and too-short vacations. And not only did we want to free ourselves from the constant stress and exhaustion of our careers, but we also had other things we'd rather spend our time doing. Every chance we got, we were making the hours-long drive from Los Angeles up to the Sierra Nevada mountains, where we'd ski in the winter and hike and climb in the summer. We felt most alive zipping open a tent in subfreezing temps at dawn from some high-altitude vantage point, taking in the sunrise in solitude. Or racing to the ski slopes before the sun rose, in hopes of grabbing that elusive first chair on a powder day. And when we were home, we loved volunteering in our community, knowing we were directly helping people in need. But as we took on more responsibility in our careers, we had less and less time to get into the mountains and into the community, and we felt work pulling us away from what we loved most.

After one too many of those early Friday nights asleep on the couch, we decided that we didn't want to live that way for another 30 or 40 years. And we made the choice to design a different kind of life: a life we'd live on our own terms, not an employer's or a client's. And so our journey to a work-optional life began, starting with a move from LA to the mountains near Lake Tahoe. I blogged about our journey to early retirement on my site, *Our Next Life*, and quickly heard from readers all over the world that they felt the same way we did. They didn't want to wait until their 60s to wrest control of their lives back from their employers. And because you're reading this now, I bet you're in the same boat.

Six years after formulating our escape plan, we waved goodbye to our careers and embarked on a new life in which we never need to work again. I had just turned 38. Mark had just turned 41. We now ski more than we ever have, and we spend time on the trails nearly every day. We volunteer much more than we could while in our careers, which replaces the sense of purpose we used to get from work, and we have time to devote to creative projects that are meaningful to us. At least once every day, I think to myself, *I can't believe this is real life.* We're so grateful to have realized that by approaching our money a little differently than most people do, we could reclaim our time and embark on the work-optional life of our dreams.

If you're willing to change your money mindset and occasionally go against what we're all taught is the "right way" to do things, you can craft the life of your dreams, too.

This book is not anti-work. Work is a good and noble thing, something nearly every person ever born has had to do in some form, whether or not they were formally employed. As humans we are wired to be productive, and work provides an outlet for that need. Work can give us a sense of purpose, a sense of contributing to society, and a sense of usefulness. The problem isn't work itself, but our current societal work culture. The culture in which too many of us wear our busyness and the bags under our eyes as status symbols. The culture that says you must hustle around the clock to be worthy. The culture that says our employers or clients own not just our work hours but every waking moment. We aren't wired to handle that.

That's why we see study after study confirming what most of us already know: Today's work culture is crushing us. Workplace burnout is at epidemic proportions,[1] and workers feel stressed and exhausted.[2] Large numbers of us work 50, 60, or even more hours every week.[3] While our parents or grandparents rarely had to take work home with them, and certainly weren't reachable after leaving the office each day, we're now expected to be connected at all times. A full half of us who use email for work check that email over the weekend. Almost as many check email when we're sick, and a third of us check work email on vacation.[4] (Is that even really vacation?) Typical senior-level employees are buried in more than 200 emails a day.[5] We feel overworked and eager to escape, even if we like the work we do.

Today we also work more overall: In 1979, Americans worked an average of 1,687 hours a year, but now log 1,836 hours. This is the equivalent of nearly four more weeks of full-time work every single year.[6] Nine out of 10 workers at all levels feel they don't have enough time to get everything done that is expected of them.[7] We're asked to do the impossible, and we no longer have enough time to unplug and protect our physical and mental health.

At the same time, we feel less secure in our jobs than ever before, even those who love their jobs and can't imagine retiring early. Many industries are being forced to adapt to technological changes and to downward price competition that result in outsourcing jobs overseas, replacing humans with robots, or closing up shop altogether. Some whole industries have gone extinct or are in danger of doing so. And other workers find themselves in occupations with a high risk of injury or disability, which could end their careers in an instant.

So it's no wonder that so many of us are craving freedom from this fast-paced, high-pressure work world. We want to work on our own terms. We want to do something slower, something healthier, something more secure—or maybe just something different, something that makes our lives feel more meaningful.

That's what *Work Optional* is all about: reclaiming your life from our nonstop work culture so that *you* decide what role work will play in your life, instead of society deciding for you.

It can take any form you imagine, from full early retirement with no paid work ever again, to a life with part-time or periodic work on your own terms. Maybe it's a life in which you escape traditional employment and go to work for yourself with a big financial safety net in place to keep the work fun instead of stressful. Or a life of full-time travel, in which you can work when and where you want. Maybe it's a service-focused life filled with volunteering or activism. It's completely up to you to define what a work-optional life looks and feels like to you. And your journey to that life is completely yours to shape, too—from what path you'll take to how fast you'll go. If you find yourself getting hung up on the word *retirement*, then choose another word. You might call what you're aiming for financial independence or financial security. Or maybe you simply call it a work-optional life. The words you choose are far less important than knowing what you want.

How to Use This Book

This isn't one of those financial self-help books that's going to push you to leap in hopes that the net will magically appear, or that's going to ignore the financial realities of the world today and pretend that anyone can make a million dollars in a month or get out of debt overnight. I'm not going to try to convince you to take big risks or promise that if you do exactly what I did, you can achieve exactly what I achieved in exactly the same way. This isn't ultimately about my journey. It's about yours. That's why the process in *Work Optional* is all about embracing *your* reality and finding *your* best options for reshaping your life. You'll come away with a solid, cautious, comprehensive financial plan, tailored to your specific circumstances, that sets you up to weather whatever future storms come your way and with a purpose-filled life plan that will keep you motivated all along your journey. If you choose to take a less cautious approach, that's cool! My goal is to empower you with all the information you need to shape your work-optional life, and to make your own choices about what's right for you and your unique situation.

Work Optional is divided into three sections. Part I is all about envisioning the life that you would be thrilled to live in early retirement, semiretirement, or a series of career intermissions, such as taking a year off from work every five years or once a decade. We'll look at what will provide you with a sense of meaning and fulfillment in lieu of a traditional career, and I'll ask you to take a close look at what you would be willing to change or give up in your life now to make that dream a reality. For example, whether you're willing to live in a smaller home, give up a car, or stop shopping for nonessentials. (Don't worry. None of that is mandatory, but the more you're willing to change, the faster you'll reach your goal.)

Part II is the financial planning portion, guiding you through the process of understanding your current spending and projecting your future spending. You will come to understand all the principles that underpin a solid early retirement financial plan, determine how much you need to save to retire or semiretire securely, create a plan and timeline to save without having to pinch pennies, and put systems into place to ensure you succeed, such as automating your saving so that you aren't continually drawing on limited willpower to set aside money each month. This section also covers strategies to speed up your progress toward your savings goal by increasing earnings and decreasing spending, perhaps by changing to a higher-paid career path or moving to a lower-cost-of-living area, and to build in contingency plans to create extra safety and security.

Part III gets back to the life part, when life after work becomes optional, planning how you'll adapt to a post-work life financially and emotionally, prioritize your well-being, and make the most of your newfound free time. Most of all, this part is about actually living your best life.

Throughout the book, I share our story so that you can see one possible route to early retirement: how Mark and I envisioned the work-optional life we wanted to live instead of the work-centered conventional one, how we built our financial plan behind that, and the completely doable steps we took to make it our reality in a short period of time. But I want you to be inspired by other possible routes as well, and that's why you'll find lots of other people's stories included here, too. Especially if you have kids, you may think a work-optional life is out of reach for you, and that's why the majority of examples included here are from parents, not from child-free people like Mark and me. From families with kids who retired early, to single people pulling it off, to couples earning under six figures combined saving faster than you might think possible, you'll see that some form of work-optional life is achievable for nearly anyone who can afford to save even a little. No matter what your circumstances are or where you're starting, you'll come away from this book with a detailed, concrete plan to make your dream of less work and more life a reality.

My hope is that, by seeing so many different paths to early retirement, you'll finish this book inspired to envision your work-optional future and pursue it doggedly, like your life depends on it. (It does!) But doing that requires hard work on your part. There are some tough questions here, like:

- What does your work-optional dream life look like in very concrete terms?
- What are you willing to sacrifice to get to that goal?
- What do you want to be able to look back on at the end of your life and know you did?

Get ready to do some introspection, to question some things you've been taught, and to consider what it might be like to walk down the road less traveled. I promise it'll all be worth it. Because there's no right or wrong way to pursue a work-optional life, only the way that's best for you.

WORK
OPTIONAL

PART I

THE WORK-OPTIONAL LIFE YOU WANT TO LIVE

Before we dig into the financial planning that will make your work-optional life possible, you need to create your vision of what you want that life to look like. Otherwise it's like driving down the highway without knowing your destination.

Get ready to dream big!

CHAPTER 1

Early Retirement:
The Ultimate Life Hack

The cost of a thing is the amount of what I call life which is
required to be exchanged for it.

—Henry David Thoreau

I was the last person anyone would have expected to retire early. A
gold star–seeking overachiever on whom the character Lisa Simpson
could have been based is not who you think would willingly walk
away from a high-powered career and a more-than-comfortable paycheck. I was the straight-A student, the editor of the school paper,
the champion mathlete (I might as well disavow you of any notions
of coolness right off the bat), the president of nearly every club I
joined. (Even chess club. Just in case you wanted to further evalu-
ate my lack of coolness.) My high school yearbook superlative was
"most likely to rule the world." Yes, I was *that girl*. And I *liked* being
that girl. I liked believing that I was doing everything right, checking all the boxes en route to the eventual work success that would
make me feel fully self-actualized and happy. I was ready to throw
myself into my career, to change the world, and to find myself in the
process. Because that's how we're taught it's supposed to work, right?

Of course, it only took me a short time in the real world to understand that things weren't going to go how I'd always expected them

to. I wasn't even in my first job yet before mentors were telling me not to follow them down their career paths—from my mentor at my dream internship at National Public Radio to my favorite professor at Berkeley. They were in positions I was positive I would feel proud to achieve one day, and they didn't seem any happier than the next guy. I was barely out of college when I realized that I could be super successful on paper and even earn loads of money, but work probably wouldn't ever fulfill me the way I'd hoped. Not that work is bad or something we shouldn't commit ourselves to, but if you're not one of the lucky few for whom work is a true calling, it's okay to aspire to do more in life than work until you die.

We're taught from our earliest schooling that there's a way we're supposed to do things: get good grades, maybe go to college, choose a career path or start a business, collect a steady paycheck, upsize our spending as our pay goes up, and stay at it all until we turn 65. Somewhere in there—the script says—we meet a spouse (or two or three), maybe have some kids, buy some new cars, pick up some hobbies and toys, go on some vacations, and then reward ourselves for all of it by playing golf all day or taking lots of cruises after we've punched the clock long enough. It's never clear when exactly the happiness or fulfillment comes, but it'll happen, *trust us*. And most of us play by the rules of the game, even though it's a fundamentally unwinnable game. No boss has ever said, "I'm promoting you and giving you a raise, and now you can work less." It's always *more*. More responsibility, more pressure, more time spent working, and more intrusion into our lives outside of work. We might get more money, sure, but we earn it the hardest way possible, by trading away our brain space and maybe even our dreams.

There's good news, though: Life doesn't have to go that way. There's an entirely different way to play the game, one that involves a much earlier exit, and it's time we reset the rules.

What Is Retirement, Anyway?

Retirement is a loaded term, filled with imagery of sitting on a beach with an umbrella drink in your hand, never doing one second of work again. But here's the thing: That's not reality for the vast majority of retirees now, nor has it been at any point in history. Retirement itself has only existed since the late 1800s, and even then, very few people actually retired. For most of human history, people have worked until they died, though that work looked almost nothing like the always-reachable, can't-get-everything-done work of today. Even in the 21st century, with more economic prosperity than ever before and more people retiring than ever before, many people don't quit working when they retire. According to the Bureau of Labor Statistics, labor force participation for adults aged 65 to 74 is increasing and will hit 32% by 2022, and 11% for those 75 and older.[1] Some of those workers are people who never retired, but many more are folks working "second acts," jobs that are often part-time and that may feel fun or purposeful. Many other retirees are redefining the term by focusing on volunteering and service, giving their retirements meaning but spending their time in ways that look an awful lot like work.

The formal concept of retirement originated in late 19th-century Prussia (now Germany) under Otto von Bismarck, and it was not instituted altruistically to give workers some well-deserved leisure time. Rather, it was put in place to force older, less-efficient workers out to make way for younger, more able-bodied workers. The retirement age was set by the economists at 70, though very few ever reached that age and benefitted from the program. Some pensions were created for military servicemen in the US and public employees like firefighters and teachers in bigger cities between the mid-19th century and early 20th century, and American Express created the first private pension in 1875, but these pensions were not meant to eliminate the need for work altogether. When the Social Security Act of 1935 was passed in the US, the retirement age was set at age 65, but at the time, the life expectancy for an American male at birth was *only* 58.[2] Most of those who reached adulthood could expect to live to age 65, but many workers would never benefit from this new program. It was instituted just after the Great Depression as an incentive for older workers to leave the workforce and make way for younger workers at a time when jobs were scarce.

Contrary to popular belief, there's also not a "correct time" to retire. Though we think of age 65 as the *right* retirement age, it was an arbitrary age chosen by economists and actuaries when Social Security was created that happened to make things balance out fiscally, not because there's anything special about turning 65.[3] And in reality, if we look at long-term trends, people are retiring far younger than we used to. In 1900, more than 60% of men 65 or older were still working, a number that dropped to 40% by 1950.[4] And by the year 2002, it was down to 17% for men, and 10% for women over 65.[5] The average retirement age currently stands at 62,[6] though nearly three-quarters of current workers say they plan to work past age 65, and two-thirds say they'll semiretire and continue to work part-time.[7] So there's no magic to any of the ages we tie to retirement—59½, 62, 65, 67, or 70½—but only functional milestones. There are other ways to fund your retirement that don't require age-linked investments, and if you build them into your financial plan, there's no reason why you have to wait for those milestone ages to leave your career.

Bottom line: Retirement is still a very recent invention. It was never intended to be something everyone could do, it certainly wasn't instituted for the good of workers (us!), and for many people it doesn't mean the end of work. Retirement is no reason to shape our entire lives in a conventional way on a made-up timeline that says we must work full-time until age 65.

The Freedom to Define Retirement for Yourself

Sociologist Robert S. Weiss defines retirement three different ways: (1) economically, by the fact that you don't need to work for money; (2) psychologically, by your own determination that you feel retired; and (3) sociologically, according to whether society sees you as retired.[8] Unfortunately, we give the last one far too much weight and think it's up to others to decide whether what we're doing qualifies as retirement. If you put yourself in a position to walk away from work—whether that's forever, temporarily, or partially—you can call yourself retired in some form if you darn well feel like it. And after you detach yourself from that arbitrary age 65 and its limiting notions of what retirement means—for example, the false notion that you're never allowed to earn another cent if you call yourself retired—you open yourself up to an entirely different way of seeing life.

Instead of using our money to buy us more things and treat ourselves to cope with the stress of working—as the standard script tells us we're supposed to—we can use that money to buy our way out of the standard work system altogether. You can hack your money and your mindset to achieve a work-optional life more quickly than most people imagine possible, reducing the role of mandatory work and increasing the time you can spend on what fulfills you most, from travel to hobbies to service to time with friends and family. Best of all, it's possible without pinching every penny or living so frugally that you make yourself miserable. Because this is ultimately about living your best life, and that means enjoying yourself both while you're saving and after you reach your goal.

While you can shape the life you're aiming for however you wish to, here are the general categories of work-optional living:

Full early retirement—You never need to work for money again. By saving enough that your investments can grow to cover your expenses forever, work becomes entirely optional for the rest of your life. There's no rule that says you're never allowed to work again if you feel inspired to do so, but with this approach, you'll never *have* to. You are financially independent.

Semiretirement—You only need to work part-time, seasonally, or in a lower-stress position. By saving enough for a traditional retirement later so that your only concern now is covering your basic living expenses, you make work something that you can do entirely on your own terms. Semiretirement can involve continuing the work you already do but on a part-time basis, or it could look a lot more like low-risk entrepreneurship, in which you start your own business but without the same pressure most entrepreneurs feel to make it hugely successful right out of the gate. You are financially secure.

Career intermission(s)—You can take a break from work for an extended period before having to go back. By saving enough to cover you for the length of your intermission, along with a buffer, you give yourself the opportunity to take a breather from work without jeopardizing your financial well-being in your later years. You can also think of this model as a self-funded sabbatical, and you might take a few of these intermissions over the course of your working years. You are financially flexible.

Noah and Becky Bouillon are a young married couple taking the career intermission approach to their work-optional life. They have saved money since their early days together in college, and thanks to scholarships, natural frugality, and work over summer breaks, they graduated from college with a few thousand dollars saved and no debt, and have continued to save money since then despite living in Seattle, a high-cost-of-living city. They do that by sharing a single car; living in a smaller house than they can afford; keeping shopping to the essentials; taking advantage of free activities like hiking, which are abundant in Seattle; and especially by travel hacking with credit card rewards.

Becky works as a labor and delivery nurse, and Noah works in software, two fields that pay above-average salaries and have a shortage of qualified employees, increasing Noah's and Becky's odds of being able to find work again quickly when their career intermission ends. Though they haven't yet saved enough to retire permanently, they've saved far more than most people their age, and they decided that their savings cushion was large enough that they could take a year-long career intermission at the ripe old age of 27, which they call their "gap year." They are traveling around North America in their car, staying in hotels they're paying for with points earned through travel hacking (more on this in part II) and camping near national parks. They are renting out the townhouse they own in Seattle while on the road and using savings and travel points to pay for the trip. Though they both feel confident that they'll be able to find new jobs again when they're ready to go back to work, having saved much more than they need for the gap year gave them the confidence to risk not being able to find work for a while.

My Journey to Early Retirement

In school, I eagerly absorbed the promise that if I worked hard and proved myself, I'd put myself on a fast-track career path to happiness and fulfillment. To me, work was never about making lots of money. It was about contributing to the greater good. And surely if I was contributing to something meaningful, that would make me happy. *Right?* Wrong. I was fortunate to do work in my career that *did* contribute good to the world, from my first internship at National Public Radio to the job I held for most of my career, as a communications consultant to political and social cause campaigns. I worked hard, I enjoyed the work, at least when it wasn't consuming every waking moment of my life, but it felt like something was still missing. All these hours I was spending at work each week were ultimately serving someone else's agenda, not mine. *That's just adulthood*, I figured, realizing that the ideas I had as a kid were wrong, and I should carry on anyway.

In my mid-20s, I met my husband, Mark, a political pollster with a seductive smile and goofy sense of humor who shares my love of the outdoors. I had recently moved from DC, where he lived, to Los Angeles, and I invited him out to California to climb Mt. Whitney, a 14,000-foot peak in the Sierra Nevada range, and those days out in the wilderness together were our *aha!* moment. While everyone around us was chasing status and stuff, we saw that we both love the outdoors and adventure above acquiring material things. Neither of us minded going days without a shower, and despite my gold star–seeking tendencies, we realized then that *this* was what we truly wanted out of life, *this* was happiness. We didn't actually need those accomplishments we'd always been taught would bring us fulfillment—never mind the fact that they never did—and instead we wanted to make our own path.

After the Whitney climb, Mark went back to DC, to a career in which he was a superstar but for which he felt ill-suited. Unlike me, Mark isn't type A by nature, but his career convinced him that he had to be, and the constant pressure to be someone he isn't wore on him. He'd much rather have been playing beach volleyball with friends or been out mountain biking, but instead put most of his free time into the job, because he felt that's what was expected of him.

Eventually Mark joined me in California, we got married, and we went about building our life together, a life that looked entirely conventional, except maybe for the absence of kids. We both worked long hours and traveled often, punctuated by trips to the Sierra whenever we could sneak away, and volunteer service when we were home in the city. Over the years, we both got a steady stream of promotions, none of which ever came with less work or with that promised happiness, and those trips into the mountains became fewer and farther between.

My dad has a rare genetic disability that forced him to stop working in his early 40s, and I'd always known that I might get the same thing one day. But "one day" felt like a long time in the future until I hit my early 30s and realized that I might only have a decade or so of full mobility left. I resolved then to make time for the things that I'd realized were truly important to me, instead of mindlessly trudging down the default path laid out in front of me.

Mark didn't need convincing. And so we embarked on our journey toward this new destination: early retirement. We moved from LA to the mountains around North Lake Tahoe, California, where our hearts told us we wanted to make our forever home, and we changed how we treated our money. Although we originally called our vision the "10-year plan," it took only six years to complete. We left our careers in late 2017 when I was 38 and Mark was 41.

To us, retiring early was never about not liking work. Work can be a source of self-worth, of community, of proof that we add value to the world. And Mark and I both got that from our careers. We just didn't want to let work be the defining feature of our entire lives, something we knew was inevitable if we didn't get on a different path. If you're like us, and you're motivated to create a work-optional life based around your values and your passions, you're in the right place.

Here's some more great news: You do not have to think of yourself as "good at money" or be in a strong financial position right now to put yourself on the path to some form of early retirement. I made *plenty* of financial mistakes when I was starting out. I spent more than I earned, on everything from cheaply made housewares to fancy groceries I didn't need. I dropped $6 a day on soy lattes from Starbucks when I barely earned enough to pay my rent. I never said no to happy hour, regardless of how little money was in the bank. I fell into the trap that so many fall into and convinced myself that getting a deal was the same as saving money. (It's not.)

I had a negative net worth until my late 20s thanks to that spending, buying a brand-new car with no down payment, and not taking my student loan balance seriously. I was too scared of losing money to invest it and kept my meager early savings in a savings account with an interest rate that didn't even beat inflation, so not only did I not earn money, I actually lost spending power.

While Mark was a little better at saving than I was, he made plenty of financial mistakes early on, too. He had a phase when he decided he needed to own a fast car, despite living in a city full of potholes, where parking is basically like driving a bumper car. He lost several thousand dollars trying to pick winning stocks that tanked right after he bought them. And he happily paid for rounds of drinks when out with friends, something that made him popular but impacted his ability to put money away.

Mark and I didn't achieve early retirement because we're better than other people at money. We did it by accepting our natural tendencies and shortcomings, and by creating systems that set us up to succeed in spite of our worst habits. We had some big advantages that made our journey shorter than some people's will be, like having gone to college, having graduated without a soul-crushing level of debt, and earning six-figure salaries in our last several working years. That last one especially accelerated our pace, but it would have been just as possible to retire early if we'd earned less, though our timeline would have been longer.

If you're in debt right now, you can still do this. If you've never invested a cent in your life and are intimidated by the stock markets, fear not. If you work for yourself and don't have an employer contributing to your retirement, a work-optional life is still within reach. I'll help you make sense of what you need to know without bombarding you with everything you don't. Whatever obstacles you're facing are things you can overcome, and we'll talk about the best ways to get past them. If you have a little money left over at the end of the month, or know you could, you can hack your own money the same way, rethinking its purpose and finding the systems that will enable you to save quickly for either your career exit or a reimagining of the work you do.

So let's debunk this myth right from the get-go: You do not need to be a magical unicorn with a computer engineering degree, earning six figures in your first job, with no student debt and no kids, and with superhero-level frugality skills to be able to retire early. Nor do you need to have started saving massive amounts of money in your 20s. Even if you are just learning about early retirement in your 50s or 60s, you likely can still achieve a work-optional life well before others retire, or at least make your traditional retirement a whole lot more secure. It's certainly true that saving money goes a lot faster if you earn more and spend less, so some people's journeys will be extremely short and others' may take 10, 15, or 20 years. Don't compare yourself to others. Instead remind yourself that most people never get to choose when they retire. Every day of freedom you can buy for yourself before age 65 is a big win and worth celebrating.

If the only thing you take away from this book is learning to look more closely at your spending, as we'll do in part II, that will still bring enormous value to your life, because doing so will allow you to better prepare for a secure traditional retirement. Retirement is a common source of worry for too many people, because they haven't saved enough, or because they *believe* they haven't.[9] Only about one in three people retire when they intend to, with the other two-thirds retiring before they feel ready because of poor health, job loss, or the need to provide care to a loved one.[10] At a time when retirement benefits and pensions are being reduced, Social Security is perennially said to be on the brink of failure, and many legacy industries are in danger of disappearing as the economy evolves, there's never been a better time to take financial planning for the future into your own hands. Removing that stress from your life will leave you feeling lighter and happier, because you'll know you've looked out for future you. And if you can take the principles in this book a little further and channel the dollars you're currently spending mindlessly into an early retirement plan that I'll help you build, you'll soon know the profound joy that comes from creating a path in life that's uniquely yours.

CHAPTER 2

Define Your Work-Optional Life

Life is too precious and short to dare to waste it on medio-
cre dreams.

—EDMOND MBIAKA

A few days into my early retirement, I woke up, went down to the kitchen, saw some Christmas cookies on the counter, and thought, "I can have a few of these for breakfast because it's Saturday." Except it wasn't Saturday. It was Tuesday. After shaking off the disoriented feeling, I reminded myself that this had been the whole point: to detach myself from the artificial time constraints that school and work had always imposed on me and get in tune with my own schedule. A wide smile spread across my face as it sunk in that I'd managed to get off the clock, literally, only a few days into my new retired life.

In early retirement, our time is truly our own. The goals I set for myself now have nothing to do with earnings or status or achievements, but with personal health and fulfillment. Mark and I can devote real time to exercise and fitness out in nature, and to cooking healthy meals from scratch. We can train to climb mountains—and then actually go climb them. I can decide I want to get better at skiing powder—and then go ski it on uncrowded weekdays, instead of battling the weekend hordes, as we always used to. He might come back scraped up and bruised, but Mark can get out on his mountain bike for hours every day in the summer if he wants. I can spend hours walking and playing with our dogs if I feel like it, guilt-free. I spend a lot of time on projects I'm excited to do for myself, like writing my blog, *Our Next Life*, and producing my podcasts, *The Fairer Cents* and *Adventures in Early Retirement*, but I also waste whole days sometimes reading on the couch or binge-watching shows I never had time for when I was constantly on the road for work.

I thought for years that the whole point of retiring early was to escape from work, but having lived it, I now realize that the real point is earning for yourself the all-encompassing sense of freedom that a work-optional life brings with it. I'm now totally free to figure out what I actually want to be when I grow up and can pursue whatever that is without money ever entering into the question. That's because early retirement isn't actually about money at all. It's about living your best life as soon as possible—complete with that indescribable feeling of true freedom—and money is merely the tool to help you do that. That's why we aren't beginning your planning process by talking about money. Leading with finances could cause you to plan a retirement based on a life that fits someone else's dream, not your own. Instead, we'll begin the planning process by walking through some questions that reveal what you truly want to get out of life. Because that's what this is all about. Living a life that makes you feel stoked to get out of bed every day and adds up to something that feels meaningful to you.

The money part of early retirement is deceptively simple in principle: Spend less than you earn, invest the difference until it generates enough money to support you forever, and then wave goodbye to mandatory work. The bigger the difference between what you earn and what you spend, the more you can save, and the faster you can retire. But the life portion—the far more important part—is significantly more complex. You need to know what your future life will cost, and to do that you need to figure out what your best and most purpose-filled life looks like. Then you'll make choices about what kind of early retirement you're aiming for and what model you want to use to pay for it (investing in real estate, index investing, dividend investing, creating passive business ventures, etc.).

Over the years of writing *Our Next Life*, I've heard from dozens of people who planned *financially* for an early retirement but didn't devote real time to planning out what their *actual life* would look like after they left work. And you know what happened? When they finally got to their work-optional life, they found that they were bored and aimless, and they went back to full-time work just because they needed something to do. That's a small tragedy. As the saying goes, "If you fail to plan, you plan to fail." Figure out your destination before you get on the road, or at least before you get too far down it. You don't have to know what every minute of every day will look like—giving yourself time to explore your brave new world is a huge part of the fun, after all—but do yourself the favor of knowing at least some of what you want to do with your newfound time before you get there.

The bonus of figuring out all the life stuff before you map out the financial plan to get you to your destination is that this well-articulated vision that you'll have created for your next life will serve as your motivation throughout the entire journey. Saving money just for the sake of saving is not nearly as much fun as knowing that every $100 or $200 that you save will buy you a day of freedom from work.

We're going to walk through some big questions here. These questions are inspiring to think about and give your inner dreamer a chance to come out and play. Some are fun and others are a bit heavier, but all of them will help you distill your varied interests and priorities in life down to what you value most and what will make you look back at the end of your life and think, *I feel good about how*

I did that. Before we begin, decide how you want to record and save your answers, because they'll come up again as we talk finances in part II. You can keep a simple list of answers, or if you like to represent things more visually, maybe your answers can take the form of a vision board. Let's dive in to the questions.

DAY-TO-DAY LIFE

- **When are you happiest?** Go back as far as your brain will let you and dig up the moments in your life when you felt the happiest and most free. What were you doing? Who were you with? Where were you? If you have a free day with nothing on the to-do list, how do you find yourself wanting to spend it? What do you daydream about when you're feeling stressed at work? What would you call your happy place?

- **What do you want to make time for every day?** Sometimes it's easier to dream big than to dream small, but think about your day-to-day life once it's no longer ruled by work. What do you want to make time for every day, or most days? Do you want to read more? Exercise more? Cook more meals from scratch? Sleep more? Have more face-to-face time with a partner or kids?

- **What are your favorite hobbies?** What are the pastimes you enjoy most? Which of them have you done for a while, and which are new? How often would you like to do them when you have more free time? Are they things you can do at home, or do they require going somewhere? Do they require special equipment? How much do they cost? Do you tend to focus on one hobby or activity, or do you like to try a variety of things?

Big-Picture Dreams

- **What did you dream of doing when you were a kid?** Did you have any career aspirations when you were growing up that you gave up on long ago? What were they? Were there experiences you dreamed of having one day that you haven't lived?

- **What would you like to accomplish in your life?** Have you always dreamed of running a marathon in all 50 states? Of adopting a dozen dogs? Of solving the hunger crisis in your city? What do you want to know you did, even if no one remembers it, to feel like you've made the most of your time?

- **What role do you want travel to play in your life?** Are you a homebody who loves nothing better than to wake up in your own bed every day, or do you dream of seeing every corner of the world? What kinds of places do you most want to visit? Are they mostly nearby or far away? How long do you envision being away from home at a time? What kind of accommodations do you want to stay in?

- **What else is on your life list or bucket list?** What are the things you want to have done before you kick the bucket? What experiences do you want to have had? What would you like to have learned? Do you have any creative goals? Spiritual pursuits?

Legacy and Purpose

- **After you're gone, how do you want to be remembered?** What kind of person do you want to be remembered as being? Is that different from how you are now? Do you want to be remembered for any accomplishments or contributions? What legacy do you want to leave behind to your descendants or to society?

- **What problems in your community or beyond do you wish you could solve?** What do you see in your day-to-day life that you wish would change? Does engaging on the issue sound fun or fulfilling to you? Do you have the urge to be more involved in your community generally? Or in advocacy or activism beyond your local community?

Self-Worth

- **Are you trying to live up to someone else's expectations?** Are there any choices you're making in your life because it's what you feel is expected of you? Is it a negative or an inspiring feeling to live up to those expectations?
- **What do you feel best at in your work?** When do you shine in your job? What skills do you have that not everyone else possesses? What are you most often praised for? Does the thought of not doing those things ever again make you sad?
- **What makes you feel best about yourself outside of work?** When do you feel most valued? What makes you feel like you matter? What contributions have you made in your family, friend circles, or community that have made you feel that you've done something worthwhile?

Central Relationships

- **Who else is a part of this vision?** Is this life you're planning just for you? For you and a partner? For you and a family? For you and close friends? For you and a hoped-for future partner and potential kids? How would you like them to be involved in the vision? Are they involved in creating it?

- **Is there anyone you wish you could spend more time with?** If you could create more free time in your life, who would you want to share it with? Are there relatives you wish you could see more? A partner? Friends? Kids? What kinds of things do you want to do with the people who are most important to you? Does it require travel to see them, or just more time?

- **What communities are you a part of that you value most?** What social circles, clubs, or other communities are you happiest in? Among whom do you have the most fun? Which communities do you connect with?

LIFE LOGISTICS

- **What kind of surroundings do you want to wake up in every day?** In your dream future, do you wake up every day where you are now? In a specific place that's somewhere else? Somewhere different every day, as part of a nomadic travel life? A new home base in another country? Write down as much about that place or those places as you imagine.

- **What timelines or milestones carry significance in your life?** Do you have aging parents you wish to spend more time with? Kids who are growing up quickly, who only have so many more years at home? An age or date at which you could receive a pension or health care benefits for life?

Now let's distill all of your answers into information that will help you craft your life vision and corresponding financial plan. First, go through your answers and circle or underline anything that jumps out at you as surprising. Second, create a summary for each category. And third, identify common themes that emerge across different categories. For surprises you identified, what makes your answers surprising? Do those surprises give you insights into how you wish to shape your life vision? Remember, this is your vision, not anyone else's, and there are no wrong answers. For the summaries and the themes, do you notice any clear priorities emerging that signal a need to shift direction in your life, or are you already heading in the direction you want to be going? Keep all of these answers in mind as we proceed.

Next, we'll figure out specifically what you value most in life, which will help you identify your top time and budget priorities in your work-optional life. The answer is in all the questions you just asked yourself and answered. Go through all of your answers and write down everything you want to do in your work-optional life, from casual hobbies to things you want to be remembered for, in no particular order. Here's an example with the answers Mark and I mapped out:

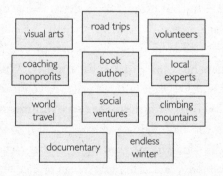

(If you're curious, "endless winter" means chasing snow around the globe to ski as much as possible for a full year. And "local experts" means developing an encyclopedic knowledge of our local trails and hidden gems.)

Next, ask yourself if there are any logical themes you can group things into. It's okay if some things don't fit into clear categories. Listen to your gut on whether the outliers don't fit thematically with other priorities because they aren't really that important to you, or because they stand alone. Discard the ones that aren't as high of a priority as your other dreams to create more space for the ones that mean the most to you. Here's ours:

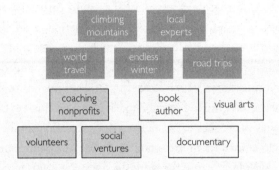

Finally, identify what those themes are.

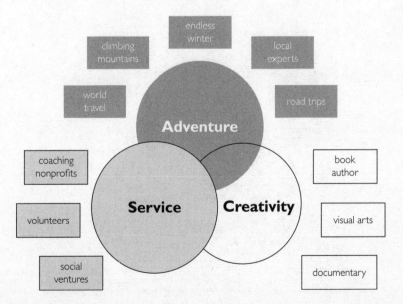

For a different example, Angela Rozmyn is a 31-year-old, married mom of a four-year-old son with a long-time passion for environmentalism. Having her son made her want to pursue a work-optional life so that she could be more present in his life. But instead of working as quickly as possible toward her financial goal along with her husband, she's made peace with taking the slow and steady approach to maintain work-life balance during her saving years. That has meant staying in a job that pays less than she could earn elsewhere, but which gives her a sense of purpose and satisfaction, a smaller workload, and more schedule flexibility, which gives her more time at home while her son is young. Being a mom has also changed some of her life priorities as well, such as having a greater interest in the community her son is growing up in. Angela is still on track to be able to retire early if she wishes to in her early 40s, even though she and her husband don't earn six figures combined. She isn't sure if she'll actually quit working, because the work she does now helps feed into her purpose, which looks different from Mark's and mine:

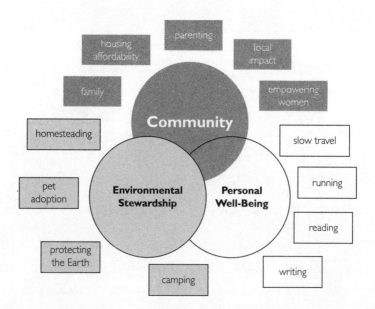

Spend some time thinking about how the things on your list cluster thematically. And then, looking at your own themes, give them a gut check: Do those themes feel right to you? If you made your entire life about the themes you identified, would that feel meaningful? Would it feel like enough? If yes, terrific! If no, what is your gut telling you? What is missing, and how does that fit in with the rest in terms of priority? If it doesn't feel quite right but you aren't sure why, sleep on it for a night or two and then come back to the questions. The point of going through these questions is not about boxing you into a to-do list for your future work-optional life, but about identifying the overarching themes and connecting threads that will give inspiration and direction to every aspect of your journey, from how you spend your money moving forward to how you derive meaning from your life without work.

While many of us imagining a life without work or with less work will tend to focus on the things we wish to subtract—namely work stress and all the time constraints—research tells us that doing only that is a recipe for unhappiness when we actually get to our destination. Even having fun every day will start to feel hollow after a while if there's not meaning behind it. The people who are happiest in life and who tend to live the longest are those who have a sense of purpose. *Purpose* doesn't have to mean anything super lofty like fixing global warming or closing the gender wage gap. *Purpose* just means that you know why you get out of bed each morning or what you want your life to add up to ultimately. Consider whether the priorities you've identified here feel like they combine to create a life you will feel proud to have lived. If not, revise as needed.

Early on in our savings journey, Mark and I worried that we were selfish to want to retire early, and sometimes the thought was strong enough to make us second-guess ourselves. Especially when you're doing something that runs so counter to the prevailing cultural norms, it's easy to get hung up on questions like whether there's something wrong with you for not wanting to do what almost everyone else does. *Are we selfish? Are we lazy? Are we bad at adulting?* We wondered about all of it. But asking ourselves what we really wanted to spend our life doing helped us see that our motivations didn't come from a selfish place. Having more time to help and serve others in our community was high on our list of early retirement priorities from the very beginning, and other aspects of the purpose were about making us better citizens of the world and better stewards of nature. Of course, our motives weren't all altruistic. We also knew we only get one shot at this life, and when we realized that it was in our power to make early retirement happen, we knew we had to go for it. Your work-optional life vision doesn't need to come from a purely altruistic place, either, but it's worth considering ways to ensure that your future life isn't all about you.

Looking at the priorities you mapped out in the last exercise, write down everything that's different from how you're currently living. Then go through your list and do the following:

- **Circle what you could change now.** For example, when Mark and I figured out that being able to get out into the mountains was our top priority, we decided to take advantage of the opportunity we had to move to Tahoe then, thanks to our remote work arrangements, and not put it off until some potentially far-off future date. But the things you could change now don't have to be as big as a move. If you dream of gardening more in the future or learning Spanish, what's to stop you from doing that now?
- **Cross out things that aren't realistic.** I'd love to climb Mt. Everest, but with asthma and some genetic mobility challenges, climbing to nearly 30,000 feet is probably not happening. While it may feel sad to cross off dreams, what you're actually doing is prioritizing things you know you'll

do and making more time and space for them. Taking Mt. Everest off my list made more time for writing and travel, which makes me happy.

- **Underline the things that feel worth making big changes in your life.** This will be your list of everything that's realistic, that you can't change now, and that you're willing to change when work is no longer an obstacle. For example, if you dream of living at the beach and you currently live far inland, are you willing to pick up and move, leaving your current friends and community behind, or if you have kids, to uproot them? Are you willing to spend more or move into a smaller space to make a move possible? If you dream of traveling the world, are you willing to cut down on frivolous spending now to save faster toward that vision? If yes, underline those things.

It may not seem like a big deal, but the exercise you've just gone through reveals what you value most in life, and that's huge! We don't often take the time to look beyond what's right in front of us and consider the big questions like this. We'll use this list again in the next chapter, as we talk about making changes in your life to set you on the path to early retirement, and then again in part II as we map out your work-optional financial plan. But for now, take a moment to sit with this vision of what you want your life to be about. Internalize it. Print it out on a piece of paper and stick it on your wall. Start telling people about it. After Mark and I mapped out our themes, we explained our plan to people as "We're planning to retire early to a life of adventure, creativity, and service." Doing that made it feel real, and it reminded us in those moments when we were tempted to spend money why we'd be happier if we saved it. Make your themes a central part of the story you tell yourself about who you are and where you're headed.

Get Your Partner (If You Have One)
on the Same Page

Mark and I were incredibly lucky that neither of us had to convince the other one that early retirement was a good idea. But that won't be true for every couple. I frequently get notes from people, most often men, asking how they can get their spouse on board with the early retirement savings plan that they've put together. And here's my answer, which might surprise you: Throw that plan out. A savings and spending plan that only one partner develops isn't going to reflect your shared vision and priorities as a couple, and it doesn't give your spouse, who hasn't contributed to it, the ability to see him- or herself in it. It's one thing to throw some rough numbers together to show your partner that early retirement is possible as a proof of concept, but if you are building out a full, detailed financial plan without your partner's buy-in, you've put the cart way out in front of the horse.

Start instead by asking each other the questions in this chapter and doing the priorities exercise together. That's useful whether you ultimately decide to pursue early retirement or not. Most of us get stuck in day-to-day tunnel vision and don't take the time to check in with our partners periodically on our larger aspirations and dreams. So ask each other: *In a world without the constraints of work, what would we want to be doing?* With luck, your answers will be similar, and it will be easy to create a shared dream and plan that you both feel inspired to aim for.

If your visions for life are wildly divergent, spend time talking through what those visions are and figuring out where they align, instead of trying to get your partner to go along with the numbers side of things. Divorce rates spike right after retirement, often because couples discover, when they finally have more time together, that they have different ideas about what they want life to be like. It's far better to figure that out now, when you have time to grow together toward a shared vision, than to coerce one partner to go along with a plan they aren't excited about.

Plan Around Kids

If you have children or plan to have them, you already know they will impact your early retirement planning in a big way. Most obviously, they cost money and will mean saving at a slower pace than you might be able to without kids. But children might also inspire you to sequence your work-optional life differently. If you want to have more time with your kids, you might decide to aim for semiretirement with part-time work while they are young, and then plan to return to full-time work when they're older. Or, if you have a partner, you may want to structure it so that you each take staggered career intermissions so that someone is home with the kids full-time in their younger years. Or you may decide to aim for a career intermission that would give you a year off of work to travel and roadschool your kids. There's no right or wrong way to do any of this. There's only the way that's best for you and your family.

Jamila Souffrant is one of those rare people who seem able to juggle everything, maintaining a high-powered corporate career while also being a devoted mom to her three kids, as well as producing a podcast and running a business on the side. But as much as she enjoyed and excelled at her job, it required her to spend three to four hours commuting every day, time that she couldn't spend working on things that brought her more happiness, and time that she couldn't spend with her children or her husband, who works as a schoolteacher. It became clear that her family and meaningful work were her top priorities in life, and that she wanted to have more time outside of work to spend with the kids while they were still young. She began saving in earnest for early retirement while working her corporate job, and, combined with her husband's teacher salary, they were on track to have the option to retire early in their late 30s. But Jamila knew she'd be miserable spending most of her time in a cubicle and missing out on that much of her kids' childhood while working and commuting, so together, she and her husband decided to change their path. Now, Jamila runs her own company from home, providing financial education and coaching services. Her leap to self-employment en route to a fully work-optional life was made possible by having saved enough to cover a few years of living expenses in addition to being on track with traditional retirement savings, so that they can weather any periods when business is slow. She doesn't know for sure if she'll actually retire early, but she expects to become fully work optional in her mid-40s on her amended path. Although that's a little slower than they had originally envisioned, she's much happier now and has full control over how much time she spends working.

CHAPTER 3

Create Your Money Mission Statement

The secret to having everything is believing that you already do.

—UNKNOWN

To achieve early retirement, you need to save a significant sum of money, a task that can sound daunting at the outset, or inspire visions of clipping coupons day and night, wearing threadbare clothes, or staying home when everyone is out having fun. But that's not what this approach is about. Saving 30¢ on a can of soup is fine, and there's no reason not to do that if you enjoy clipping coupons, but it's not a plan to get you enough funds for retirement. Instead, we're taking the non-penny-pinching approach to saving that's focused on getting the biggest bang for your buck, playing to your strengths, spending only on what you value most, and recognizing the most common spending pitfalls that derail people's savings goals. Though it may seem hard to believe, if you've never been a saver before, saving large sums is entirely possible if you make the choice to change your money mindset. There was a time when I wouldn't have believed it, but I have since seen it with my own eyes.

Every few months, a news story comes out about some family

earning six figures who feels like they're just scraping by. You've probably seen the headlines. The family in Manhattan earning $500,000 a year who lives paycheck to paycheck. The tech worker in San Francisco making $200,000 who feels broke because the cheapest apartment she can find costs $6,000 a month. These stories always elicit plenty of well-deserved eyerolls from the vast majority of people who manage to get by just fine on a whole lot less than those folks. But I'll confess: I understand how this happens, because we experienced a taste of it before we got serious about saving. The culprit is *lifestyle inflation*. In our later earning years, Mark and I were each making six figures, and most of our peers were doing the same. And over the decade or two that we'd all been at this whole adulting thing, expenses had slowly and sometimes invisibly creeped in for most of our friends: The $100 cable bill came first, and then $100 cell phone bills became the norm. The $75-a-week house cleaner feels like a necessity and not an extravagance when you can barely keep yourself clothed and fed with your busy work schedule. Then maybe your car dies and you decide you'd rather have a new one than a used one. You have a kid and now need to pay for daycare so you can still go to work and earn that paycheck. With three of you, your apartment feels too cramped and you decide you need a house instead, but in the expensive city where you live, that means taking on a huge mortgage (if you can afford to buy a house at all). And with the car seat, that efficient car you only bought a year ago feels too cramped, so you decide to upsize to an SUV. You look around you and see everyone else making the same choices, so you assume it's just inevitable to spend as much as you're spending. And on and on it goes. Each vacation slightly nicer than the last, a few more luxuries here and there, but it's all okay because you work hard and *deserve* some conveniences, right?

No one of those expenditures on its own feels over-the-top or like the thing that will stop you from being able to save money. But they gradually pile up, and if you aren't subtracting expenses as you add new ones, you wake up one day and realize that your life—a life that just feels *normal*—is expensive to maintain. The more expensive your life is, the harder it is to save money. Mark and I avoided a lot of common forms of lifestyle inflation, but where it hit us hard was restaurant spending. When you're both exhausted from working a long day, it's tempting to hand over a little cash in exchange for someone else doing the cooking and dishes. Sometimes we paid for dinner five times a week, but it never seemed like a problem, because we didn't go straight from cooking every meal at home to buying most dinners out. It happened gradually, and we never perceived the shift. A dinner out here and there turned into dinners out regularly, which turned into dinners out regularly with a few takeout dinners thrown in, which turned into dinners out regularly with takeout dinners most other nights. The slippery slope from one into the next was invisible, but when we finally thought to pay attention, we realized we were spending a fortune on food. Or think about Carrie Bradshaw on *Sex and the City* and all her $400 shoes. It's hard to imagine she went from buying shoes at Payless one day to buying Manolos and Jimmy Choos the next. Most likely, she gradually worked her way up the price ladder, with each step not feeling like a significant enough difference to warrant concern. It's this invisible slippery slope that makes lifestyle inflation the single biggest threat to early retirement, a fact backed up by research. Only a third of people in the US follow a detailed budget, while two-thirds don't budget or track their spending closely, nor do they follow a big-picture financial plan.[1]

Lifestyle inflation is a phenomenon that affects people at all income levels and is the result of a psychological phenomenon called hedonic adaptation, which is the tendency we all have to adapt quickly to changes in our lives and return to a baseline level of happiness, regardless of how many good or bad things may happen. Put in purchasing terms, it means that if we set our sights on a new car because we think that will make us happier in some way, we may get an initial happiness boost from buying it, but pretty soon, we're no happier with the car than we would have been without it—though we're definitely shorter on cash as a result. Financial experts talk about this as the hedonic treadmill, or the idea that we are always running toward something—usually material things we wish to buy—but never making real forward progress in terms of happiness. Yet most of us continue to chase happiness while actually running in place, thinking we'll catch it when we get that next promotion, receive that next raise, or make that next big purchase. Of course, we never do.

It's worth taking some time to think about what your life looks like today compared to what it looked like a few years ago or in your very early working years to identify how your lifestyle has inflated. Examine what you spend money on now that you didn't used to spend on and which of those additions truly make your life better. Consider which of those new expenses cover true needs, like school expenses for kids, and which cover wants, expenditures that aren't necessary but are purely optional. Most lifestyle inflation tends to happen with wants masquerading as needs. For example, many people require a car to get to work. If we consider all cars equal, then it's easy to justify trading in for a brand-new car every few years because a car is clearly a need. However, all cars are not equal, and a *new* car is not a need. A cheap, used, 20-year-old car will get you to work just as effectively as the nicer car, so the used car is the need, a newer car is a want masquerading as a need, and a string of newer cars over the years is textbook lifestyle inflation keeping you from saving as much as you could. Even a seemingly small expense that costs only $20 a week adds up to more than $1,000 a year, money you might be able to save instead. You're allowed to have things in your life that you want, but if your goal is to retire early, one of the best things you can do for yourself is to learn to recognize when your lifestyle is inflating, to sniff out the wants pretending to be needs, and to be deliberate about the lifestyle inflation you choose to spend money on.

The second biggest barrier to saving, related to lifestyle inflation, is mindless spending, those seemingly small expenditures we make every day without thinking, most often on things that don't add real value to our lives. Mindful spending is spending you plan for and consider thoroughly before handing over your hard-earned cash, spending where you make sure you really need that thing or at least that you'll use it often enough to justify the cost.

When you spend mindfully, you're truly using money as it should be used: as a tool that provides for your basic needs and your top priorities, things that make your life better. But fighting you in your mission is all of the mindless spending that we let creep into our lives, often without noticing—every impulse buy, every subscription or membership you forget about but keep paying for, every bit of convenience you pay for in the moment that you didn't really need. If you spend $10 on lunch at work every day, one meal doesn't feel like it will make or break you financially. But if you add that up for all the work days in a year, that's $2,400 you've spent without realizing it. If you'd made your lunch instead, you could have spent a fraction of that.

There's no category of spending that's inherently mindful or mindless; the test is how it improves or doesn't improve your life. Using that lunch example, if you never go out to eat otherwise, you savor each bite of the lunch you buy, and the experience gives you a much-needed respite from work stress that lets you get through your day, then maybe that $2,400 a year is entirely worthwhile. Likewise, if you're so busy with work and kids that not having to prepare your own lunch gives you relief from what would otherwise be a huge source of stress, then it very well may be money well spent—but you could probably also find a way to trim the daily cost down a bit. If, however, you know you could figure out a way to prepare your own lunch, and you rush through it each day, barely tasting it, then it's mindless spending in your case, and it's an obvious place to cut.

Eliminating unnecessary sources of lifestyle inflation and mindless spending from your life is the most painless way to find money you could be saving instead of spending, and it should be your first step. But to save even more without sacrificing everything you enjoy, it helps to change how you think about money. When we first encounter money as children, it's often as a reward. Perhaps we find a crisp bill in a birthday card from Grandma, or we receive a few dollars in exchange for doing our chores. We learn very early on that money can buy us the things we want, like the toy we saw on TV or the candy our parents won't buy us. And we carry that belief into adulthood, using money to treat ourselves for working so hard or to make life more convenient. But that act of purchasing something we want is not the main transaction that happens with our money. The first and most important transaction is what gets that money in the first place: work. We trade our time, energy, and brain space for a paycheck. In essence, we've already paid for the money itself by the time it arrives in our hands.

And we can continue to trade it away for things we may or may not need, or we can begin to see money for what it truly is: a repository of the time we put into earning it, a concept originated by Vicki Robin and Joe Dominguez in *Your Money or Your Life*. When we recognize that the money we earn can in turn be used to buy back our future time, it's suddenly much easier to determine what feels worth our money and what doesn't.

If a new shirt costs as much as you earn in three hours, then it really costs three hours of your life, three hours you will never get back. That's the immediate cost. But the cost in the long run may be even greater. Every dollar you can avoid spending per week is at least $300 you don't have to save for retirement, whether that's early retirement or traditional retirement (we'll discuss this in chapter 7). And if you earn more now than you expect to need in retirement, then the true cost of something is not only the amount of life that you exchanged for purchasing it, it's also the opportunity cost of even more life that you'll have to spend at work rather than having that time to do as you wish.

After you calculate the cost of your future life in part II, you can divide the annual number by 365 to put an actual price tag on a day of early retirement. When faced with spending what might seem like an inconsequential $150 on something or banking that money to cover a day or more of future freedom, your decision-making becomes much simpler. It becomes simpler still when we remind ourselves that we can always make more money, but our time is in finite supply. Reorient your thinking about money to see it as a repository of the time you spent earning it and a tool to buy that time back, instead of as a means of rewarding yourself for your work. Saving money just to save it isn't much fun unless you're one of the rare few who is naturally frugal, but when there's a clear reason for saving, it's amazing how different saving money feels.

Of course, talking about lifestyle inflation, mindless spending, and changing how we see money are all about *not* spending. But spending isn't inherently bad. Spending on the things you truly value is the best thing you can possibly do with your money. As Mark and I got clear on our vision for our work-optional life, the way we spent money transformed almost overnight. With this new mindset about money, we scaled back on restaurant meals immediately, and we cut out whole categories of expenses like cable TV, new ski gear, and the not-so-occasional bottle of wine we'd taken to buying and saved that money instead. And because we knew why we were saving, we didn't miss any of those things. Travel, by contrast, was something that was too important to us to give up, and we'd both get uncomfortable whenever one of us suggested not taking a trip so that we could save a bit faster. That made clear to us that travel was one of our top priorities and therefore an area where spending should not be a question. But, just as wants sometimes masquerade as needs, unnecessary expenses during travel often sneak into our spending. We then agreed we cared most about being able to experience places, not what the thread count was of the sheets we were sleeping on. We worked out a compromise by making our trips fit within a smaller budget, even if that meant staying in a shoebox of a hotel room or taking a bus instead of a plane.

Anyone can save a high percentage of their income if they spend nothing. But a life in which you spend nothing or pinch every penny to spend as little as humanly possible is not likely to be a life that feels worth all the effort you put in at work. The trick is to find the right balance for you between spending and saving based on the priorities you identified in chapter 2. You likely already know what expenditures are nonnegotiable, though you may decide you're happy to reduce the costs associated with them without losing the core experience. But even after rooting out lifestyle inflation and mindless spending, there's probably still a lot of gray area in your budget, because we're all only human. Temptation happens. We run out of willpower and make an impulse buy, or we succumb to consumer marketing and convince ourselves we need some new gadget. The best way to guarantee your success at saving the money you want to save is, first, to make up your mind that you're going to save more money. Just as you're rewriting your personal narrative to include your life's top priorities, expand it to include the fact that you are someone who saves money, even if that's an entirely new concept in your financial life. It's never too late to change. And if the concepts of lifestyle inflation and the hedonic treadmill resonate with you, write into your new narrative that not only are you a person who saves, you're also someone who avoids chasing temporary happiness or status with your spending. And second, give your money a mission statement that ensures it does exactly what you want it to do.

When it comes to sticking to financial goals, simple is virtually always better. The more you can simplify your decision-making, the less you rely on your limited stores of willpower when mulling over whether to buy something. A money mission statement does exactly that, outlining a spending philosophy that's aligned to your priorities—meaning that you choose to spend money mindfully on purchases that truly add value to your life, and you decline to spend money on everything else. It also provides guidance on spending triggers to avoid and communicates your overarching goal. To help determine the spending philosophy that you wish to incorporate into your money mission statement, let's walk through some thought-starter questions. Just as you did in chapter 2, write down your answers so that you can identify common themes, and if you have a partner, make sure to engage them and answer these questions as a team.

- **What is the single best thing you've ever spent money on?** You might immediately know the answer to this, but if you don't, go back to the happiest memory you identified in chapter 2. What were you doing? What did it cost? How has spending that money brought you a lasting happiness boost and not just a quick dopamine rush before you returned to the hedonic treadmill? Did spending that money make your life easier in some way? More fun? More interesting? Did it give you memories that you treasure? How, specifically, did that spending benefit you?

- **What ongoing expenditure makes you happiest?** Of all the money you spend regularly, what portion of that gives you the biggest ongoing happiness boost? What about it makes you happy? How does it improve your life?

- **What do you spend money on that you wouldn't miss?** What are some things you currently purchase or pay for that you know you'd be fine living without? Especially thinking about some of the mindless or impulse buys most of us make, what could you cut out of your life relatively painlessly? What do you spend money on now that you haven't always spent money on that you could subtract without major sacrifice?

- **What would feel like too big of a sacrifice to be worth it?** What spending feels completely nonnegotiable to you, no matter how wonderful that future best life vision feels? What, if you gave it up, would make the end goal not feel worth it?

- **Could you spend less on the things you value without missing out on the core of the experience?** Thinking about the expenditures you value most, do they have to cost as much as they cost now? Could you find ways to get more or less the same experience, but spend less? If you love running, could you ditch your gym membership and only run outside? If you love family holiday celebrations, could you scale back on gift giving while still enjoying the time together just as much?

- **Was there a time in your life when you enjoyed your lifestyle but spent less than you do now?** Think back at different stages of your adult life and what the circumstances were at each stage. Was there any prior stage of your life when you spent less but were just as happy, or perhaps even more happy? Could you go back to that level of spending and give up some of the more recent ways your lifestyle may have inflated?

- **Is there anything you enjoy but are willing to give up to reach your goal?** Do you have any expensive hobbies you could swap for something cheaper? Do you love your home but know you could be happy in a smaller one? Do you relish driving a fast car, but know you could get around just as well in an economical used car? If you live in a city with good transit, could you live without a car altogether? Do you love wearing trendy clothes but know you could save more if you stuck to basics that you could wear for several years? What are you willing to trade away to be able to get to your work-optional life more quickly?

Now that you've answered all the questions, do the same thing we did to identify your life priorities: Look for the common themes in what's most important to you, what you could eliminate from your life without missing it, and what you could still enjoy but while spending less. Make special note of anything that surprised you. Next, look back at those life priorities you identified in chapter 2, and ask yourself how well they line up to the spending priorities here. Is there any category of expenditure that feels dramatically different? Could you cut or at least scale back that expenditure category? It's okay if the answer is no, particularly if we're talking about expenditures that are necessary to be able to do your work and earn a paycheck. For spending in that category, flag it as an expenditure you can eliminate after you're no longer living a work-mandatory life.

Finally, combine all of this into a spending philosophy by filling in the following statements:

I spend mindfully and without guilt on:
I spend only as much as necessary on:
I do not spend money on:

In some ways, that last line is the most powerful because it eliminates the question altogether. The next time you're faced with the choice of spending money on something on that list, you won't have to waste any time thinking about it because you know that's not how you spend, or it's not how you spend anymore. It's like asking a vegetarian if they want a steak. They don't have to stop and think about it, because they already know the answer. Automating your decision-making like this is one of several systems we'll put in place to ensure you succeed in achieving your version of early retirement.

The next element of your money mission statement is an examination of your spending triggers. Though most of us engage in some level of mindless spending, you don't have to be a shopaholic or problem spender to benefit from a closer examination of your spending triggers. Understanding when, why, and how you tend to spend money will make it easier to spend less and save more as you embark on your early retirement journey. When I started paying closer attention to our spending, one of the things I noticed immediately is that I never had a transaction at Target in which I spent less than $100. I'd go in with a relatively short list of things we needed but would somehow always end up with much more in the cart. None of it felt extravagant, but over time that lamp here, new curtain rod there, or cute serving dish on another trip added up to thousands of dollars. I quickly realized that Target was a spending trigger for me. If you know your spending triggers and can train yourself to avoid them, you'll be amazed how much easier it becomes to save money. So let's identify what they are.

Ask yourself how you spend money. Do you tend to:

- Shop without a list?
- Buy more than what's on your list?
- Shop online frequently?
- Subscribe to things and then forget about them?
- Buy things "just in case you need them" at some future date?
- Shop as a hobby or when you're bored?
- Buy more than you meant to at certain stores or on certain websites?
- Look to upgrade what you already have (home, cars, electronics, etc.) whenever you have the chance?
- Buy things in bulk, even when you don't need that much?
- Buy things you don't need when you get a sale notice or coupon code?

- Buy something simply because it was on sale or seems like a good deal?
- Go grocery shopping when hungry?
- Buy many options of something, intending to return all but one?
- Buy what's trendy?
- Buy what you see friends or neighbors wearing or using?
- Spend money on experiences like dining out without keeping track of how much you're spending?
- Spend more when you're with others?
- Spend more when you're alone?

The point of asking these questions isn't to judge the spending but to identify the behaviors that trigger you to spend more than you intend to. When you know what your triggers are, you can take steps to avoid them so that you stay on track with your saving and keep your money working according to its mission. If you have a partner, each of you should think about this list and the checklist below. Two partners may have the same values and priorities, but money is such a personal, emotional thing that each of us may have very different spending triggers and emotional responses to money. Target was a trigger for me, but for Mark it was seeing his friends on new skis or on a new mountain bike. He wanted their cool new toys and would dream about how much better he would be at that activity if only he had what they had.

The list above represents the functional triggers that may lead you to spend more than necessary, but spending is often triggered as an emotional response, and you may find that some of your spending triggers have more to do with feelings than with being in a particular place or having certain habits.

For example, many of us spend money to buy things that we

think will make us better versions of ourselves, like buying a bicycle in hopes that it will turn you into a regular cyclist, purchasing an expensive carry-on bag expecting that you'll become a more frequent traveler, or buying more books than you'll ever read because you like the idea of being the type of person who would read those books. Marketers are wildly skilled at making us buy in to the mythical tales they tell, enticing us to spend hundreds of dollars on new phones that will mark us as savvy or cool, even when our old phones work perfectly well, or convincing us that this new pair of shoes will make us run faster. This type of spending is often called "keeping up with the Joneses," which is spending money to project a certain image that we think society or our neighbors expect, or even to change how we see ourselves. If you engage in this, you're in the majority, but you don't need to stay there.

Other signs of emotional spending are buying things when you feel stressed out or overwhelmed by negative emotions, sometimes in the name of "self-care"; buying things to fill emotional holes; buying something only to find that you had bought almost exactly the same thing previously or discovering that you bought something you don't remember purchasing; and spending money because we feel it's expected of us, not because we actually value the thing we're spending on. Most of us spend at least some money that we feel we're expected to spend, whether it's on birthday presents for kids' parties or to take part in an activity because someone else wants us to. But note if any of that spending in particular makes you feel resentful or coerced.

The converse behavior is important as well: spending money on people to show your love. If that's something you do, could you convey the same sentiment without spending that money or by spending less, for example, by calling them, spending time with them, or doing things for them instead?

Ask yourself which of the following emotional money decisions you sometimes make, and if you have a partner, ask him or her to do the same:

- ☐ Spend money on things that you think will make you a better or different person
- ☐ Spend money because you are stressed or overwhelmed by other emotions
- ☐ Buy stuff that you later forget you bought
- ☐ Spend money because others expect it, not because it adds value to your life
- ☐ Spend money on kids or others to show your love
- ☐ Spend money to fill an emotional void

Combine any emotional spending triggers you noted here with functional triggers in the checklist above to give you a full sense of where you want to make a point of being more mindful moving forward, which could mean altering some of your habits to avoid your functional and emotional spending triggers or finding other ways to cope. When I realized that setting foot in Target was a spending trigger for me, I tried a bunch of different ways to rein things in. I tried giving myself pep talks that I'd only buy what was on my list. And I tried going in with only cash, no credit or debit cards. But ultimately I realized that the only way to stop spending more than I meant to at Target was to stop going to Target. I made a new rule for myself that I just don't set foot in there, and you know what? The world didn't end, I found other ways to get the household staples we used to purchase there, and I don't even miss it. It's now been five years since I've shopped at Target, and my wallet is happier for it. In Mark's case, he made a deal with himself that he's allowed to trade up for newer gear like bikes and skis every few years, but he can only buy used equipment, which is much less expensive but still feels like an improvement over what he had been using.

We made other changes to our habits, too, like forcing ourselves to stop thinking of shopping as something we do, always grocery shopping with a list, and making a rule that we can buy something online only if we've had it in our cart for a full week so we have time to reflect on whether it's really a worthwhile purchase. We also got ruthless about unsubscribing from every email list we used to be on that would tempt us with sales and coupon codes. It's incredible how much it helps simply to remove the temptation. Doing all of that has cut way down on those little impulse buys that add up, kept us off of that hedonic treadmill, and allowed us to boost our savings in a big way.

As you consider what changes you will make in your life to reach your early retirement goal, it helps enormously to have a written statement you can refer back to at any time to keep you on track or revisit if you ever veer off the path. So let's put all of your reflections together into your full money mission statement. Looking at everything you said you'd spend money on with no guilt, everything you said you'd spend money on within reason, things you said you'd stop spending money on altogether, the situations that trigger spending, and the emotions that make you spend more, compile a list of the following:

- Spending
- Situations to avoid
- Emotional triggers to notice
- Habits to stop

Then come back to your life priorities, and add those:

- Highest priorities
- Mindful spending that supports my life vision

Finally, write your money mission statement, combining all of these elements and focusing especially on your big-picture vision, so you always know why you're doing this. Some examples:

My money's mission is to provide for my life of service, adventure, and creativity, eventually allowing me to retire early and stop working for money. To support that mission, I will stop shopping online without a list, I will stop shopping at Target, and I'll notice when I'm spending aspirationally in hopes that a product will make me better in some way. And I'll be more mindful about the money I do spend on adventures so I get the full experience without spending more than I must.

My money's mission is to enable me to travel more and spend more time with my kids, made possible by saving enough to scale back my time at work. To support that mission, I will stop buying the kids toys and clothes they don't need and didn't ask for, I will delete my credit card numbers from Amazon and other sites so that it's not so easy to make impulse purchases, and I will notice when I'm spending money to keep up with the neighbors.

After you've written your money mission statement, do another gut check. Have you captured your life vision, and is that reflected in how you'll treat your money from now on? How does thinking about your money mission statement make you feel? If you feel empowered, terrific! If you feel anxious, don't worry. This is your journey, and no one is going to force you to give up anything you don't feel ready to give up. Ask yourself what you do feel ready to change, even if it's just one small thing, and go from there. You may very well find that it feels easier to trim back your spending over time. Whichever the case, you'll be on the path to your work-optional life.

We've spent part I dreaming big and digging into the emotional aspects of creating a work-optional life, all of which affects how you'll shape your path to early retirement. Next we'll dig into the money itself, and get you moving on your journey.

PART II

THE FINANCIAL PLAN FOR YOUR WORK-OPTIONAL LIFE

Now that you have your life vision in place, it's time to create the financial roadmap that will get you there as quickly and directly as possible, without having to pinch pennies, be a math whiz, or sacrifice your quality of life—because that's just as important as the future you're planning for yourself.

CHAPTER 4

Invest to Fund Your Future

Good investing is boring.
—GEORGE SOROS

We seem to have a collective mental block as a society against thinking about money, especially long-range financial planning. As a result, many of us carry around the misconception that planning for your financial future is a complex, math-heavy endeavor. It doesn't have to be. As we talked about in part I, so much of how we live with money is emotional, and our ability to save it is highly influenced by our money mindset. In examining yours, you've already done the hard introspection that will make the actual financial planning a simple matter of filling in blanks, not an exercise in high-level calculus.

With that in mind, let's talk about tools or, more specifically, how to turn your money into a tool that works for you instead of you working for it. The most important thing you'll do to achieve your version of early retirement is invest your money so that it will fund your work-optional life. If you aren't already investing, don't let the idea scare you. Many financial pros purposely try to make investing sound confusing exactly so you'll hire them to manage your money for you. But the truth is if your investment approach is too complicated to explain to a child, it's probably also not a very good one. The best investing strategies are boring and easy to understand. They're also simple to implement on your own.

So that you're well equipped with the knowledge you need to choose which investments you want to incorporate into your early retirement financial plan—which tools you want to include in your tool set that will do the work for you—let's first talk about the principles that make every form of early retirement possible. Everyone who's ever had a job understands the idea of earning money. You go to work, and every two weeks or so, a paycheck arrives, rewarding you monetarily for the time and effort you put in. Or you own your own business, you bill clients, and the payments for the work you do for them arrive. Technically speaking, that's called earned income. For most of us, that's the only way we're taught to make money. But it's also entirely possible to focus on shifting from earned income to the confusingly named unearned income, which really just means money you receive without having done any labor. This is made possible in part through the wonder that is compound interest. You may also hear this money called passive income, but I prefer to call it magic money.

There's no actual magic involved, of course, but when you watch money you've invested grow and multiply over time, without you doing a thing, it sure feels like magic. The "magic" is really just the compounding of interest, capital gains, and asset appreciation earned on money you've invested, meaning that what you earn each year is multiplied on top of prior years' growth, not just added, making the growth happen much faster. If you can invest enough, eventually you have enough magic money or passive income spinning off of your invested assets that it covers all of your living costs, meaning you don't need to work anymore, or you can work much less. Regardless of which form of early retirement you're interested in pursuing—full early retirement, semiretirement, or career intermission—the principle is the same: You want to invest as much as possible, as early as possible, in investment vehicles that will grow to give you a steady stream of income for life, long after you've stopped relying on mandatory work to provide for you. And those income streams keep coming whether you ever lift a finger (magic!), freeing you up instead to spend your time on more meaningful pursuits outside of normal employment and entrepreneurship structures.

The math behind early retirement—invest enough by spending less than you earn to generate enough magic money to support you—is something anyone can understand. But behaviorally, succeeding on your quest to achieve a work-optional life means doing the opposite of what nearly everyone else does. Most people earn their incomes actively but plan their financial lives passively. That is, they go to work every day to earn a paycheck, but don't pay enough attention to their financial big picture and end up feeling powerless about their money and unprepared for retirement, if they can ever afford to retire at all. Pursuing some form of early retirement is fundamentally about flipping that equation upside down: planning your financial life actively and earning your income passively. Or, again, magically.

There are any number of possible combinations of tools you can use to build magic money streams, which we'll discuss below, but most people planning for a work-optional life will put the majority of their focus into one of four basic approaches:

1. **Drawdown investing:** Investing in stocks and bonds, either individually or through mutual or index funds, that the investor expects to grow in value over time, so that they can sell (draw down) shares for more than they paid for them, with the proceeds of selling shares becoming their primary magic money.

2. **Dividend investing:** Investing in stocks or stock mutual funds of companies that pay large dividends (a portion of

corporate profits paid out to shareholders) relative to the companies' share prices, so that the investor receives magic money in the form of those dividends without having to sell shares. Dividend investors can also later sell shares, with the proceeds serving as additional income.

3. **Rental real estate investing:** Buying real estate to rent out, with the net profit earned after subtracting expenses from the rent collected serving as semi-magic money. ("Semi-magic" or "semi-passive" because managing rental real estate can be quite time-consuming. But there are ways around that, as we'll discuss later.) Real estate investors can also sell properties, and any money made from increased property values is additional magic money, though it may be subject to hefty taxes.

4. **Passive business income generation:** Investing time to build a business that generates magic or semi-magic income through minimal effort on the part of the business owner. In some cases, the business may later be sold to a new buyer, with those proceeds providing a one-time infusion of magic money, but at the cost of a regular income stream thereafter.

Though the investing methods differ, the goal behind all of these approaches is fundamentally the same: The investor (you) puts hard-earned money into their chosen investment vehicles with the expectation that the magic money generated from the investments will increase faster than inflation and expenses. Therefore, the value of your investments and the profit from them grows over time, which will allow the investments to provide enough magic money to support you for your entire lifetime. To put that another way: You don't have to save every dollar that you will ever need to live on. If you invest your money wisely, the markets, your tenants, or your customers will fund a lot of that growth for you, meaning you'll get to your ultimate goal more quickly than you might imagine possible.

Everything You Need to Know About Investing (Which Is Not a Lot)

If the idea of investing at all is intimidating to you, you are not alone. Even after I started to develop good financial habits and save more money, I kept it in a regular savings account for way too long. The idea of that FDIC insurance—the federal guarantee that you won't lose money up to $250,000 kept in savings accounts—was so comforting, and investing to me meant the possibility of losing everything. The idea of having to choose the right stocks was terrifying, too. *How could I, a regular person, possibly know how to pick winning stocks?* I wondered. *I don't know how to read a corporate earnings report or assess share price relative to market capitalization. I don't even know what* market capitalization *means!* (You don't actually need to know it either, but it's just the stock's share price times the number of shares.) I wasn't alone in my fears. Currently, only a third of those under age 35 invest in stocks, and many are wary of stock market investing, no doubt as a direct result of the 2008 financial crisis.[1] It took me a few years to break out of the mindset that only investment professionals can understand this stuff, but as I did more research and built my knowledge, I realized that you really only need to know a few key facts to get comfortable with investing and to do it successfully. If all you know about investing is these three points, you'll still have all the knowledge you need to reach your goals:

1. **You don't have to beat the markets by picking the right stocks. You just have to *match* the markets.** Historically, US stock markets average annual gains of 9–10% before inflation, and 6.8% after inflation, which is plenty to make your portfolio grow enough to sustain you for a long retirement. And it's actually easy to match the markets exactly if

you avoid trying to pick winning stocks and invest primarily in index funds, which track either the full US stock market or key indices like the S&P 500.

2. **You don't have to be lucky with timing to do well in the markets.** Over every 10-year period in US stock market history, markets have been up from where they were a decade earlier, even when you adjust for inflation. And study after study has shown that it's much more important to give your money time to grow in the markets than it is to get lucky with timing. (And anyone who insists that market timing is about skill, not luck, is trying to sell you something. Run far, far away.) As the saying goes, "Time in the markets is more important than timing the markets." The nature of the markets is to go up and down, so you do need to get used to the idea that sometimes your accounts will look like they've lost money. But you only lose money when you sell shares and lock in your losses, so if you buy and hold for the long term, those short-term fluctuations don't matter, and you're better off tuning them out. So long as you don't need the money you're investing in the markets right away, you're virtually guaranteed that it will gain in value over time. And as a smart investor, you're only interested in the long term. Any money you need in the short term, such as an emergency fund or money to buy a home, should be saved outside of the markets in cash savings vehicles.

3. **Inflation may be a bigger threat to your money than market risk.** Since the 2008 financial crisis, "high-interest" savings accounts have yielded between 0.5% and 1.75% annual interest on the money saved there. Meanwhile, inflation has averaged between 2% and 3%, which is consistent with the historical average of 3.3%, and with the US Federal Reserve Bank's goal of keeping inflation around 2%. So if you save

$1,000 for a year in a high-interest savings account, at the end of the year, it might be worth $1,015 (1.5% APR) at the high end, but thanks to inflation, it now takes $1,030 (assuming 3% inflation) to buy what a thousand dollars would have bought you a year ago. In other words, if you're parking all your money in savings accounts, you are *guaranteeing* that you're losing spending power. This is called inflationary risk. The dollars may not actually be getting smaller in number, but any savings or investment vehicle that isn't beating inflation is a losing investment. If you'd instead invested that $1,000 in a low-cost index fund, historically it would average around 9% in gains, 6–7% gains after inflation, assuming you had reinvested the dividends, and while that number will vary year to year, you can count on your spending power growing over the long term with market investments.

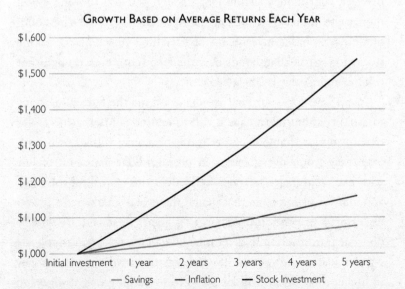

GROWTH BASED ON AVERAGE RETURNS EACH YEAR

A big part of getting comfortable with investing is getting comfortable with risk, and the best way to do that is to accept that there's truly no such thing as a risk-free path. It's just a matter of which risk you choose. The idea of retiring early carries with it the risk that you *could* run out of money one day, but working until you're in your 60s isn't risk-free, either. First, folks who work until their 60s regularly undersave for retirement and also risk running out of money. But more importantly, they risk spending all their best years at work instead of using those years to pursue their own passions and enjoy time with those they care most about. Plenty of people live healthy, active, vibrant lives into their 60s and 70s, but it's certainly no guarantee. Buying bonds is another choice that feels like the lower-risk option, in relation to buying stocks, but bonds come with their own risk in the form of lower yield: Morningstar analysis shows that large company stocks outpace government bonds by an annual average of more than 4 percentage points (9.8% to 5.7%), an enormous difference over an investing lifetime that could easily be the difference between your money lasting long enough and you running out of money late in life. Over the long term, stocks give you the best odds of all market-based investments of stretching your dollars, making stocks lower risk than bonds over the long term, even though they can lose more value in any given year.

As an investor, your goal is not to fall for the fallacy of trying to avoid risk, but to manage it and to remind yourself as necessary that any option that looks "safer" probably comes with its own risks. Stay away from investments that promise huge gains out of line with market averages, as those are likely scams or wishful thinking, and aim for investments that match the overall markets. In investing, average is good, just as boring is good. That said, it's wise to do some introspection to determine how much risk you can tolerate without it stressing you out. If you know that investing your money in higher-risk vehicles will keep you from sleeping well at night, an aggressive investment strategy of 100% stock and stock funds is probably not for you. And conversely, if you don't mind watching your account balances bob up and down a bit, then a more conservative strategy with a high percentage of bonds and cash wouldn't suit you very well either. Every type of asset comes with its own risk profile, and in general, the more an investment stands to gain, the more it also stands to lose. But there are other ways to manage risk tolerance that aren't strictly focused on which investment vehicles you choose. So keep an open mind as we walk through your investment tool options.

In addition to paying attention to risk profiles, fees should be high on your list of things to look out for. Investment fees, which go by names like *expense ratios, management fees, loads, sales fees,* or *trading fees,* can quickly erode your portfolio gains if you aren't careful, even when they seem innocuous. Consider an investment with a 2% annual expense ratio that nets gains of 8% per year on average. That 2% may seem small, but it's a full quarter of the 8% gains you would have made without the fee. Now, your 8% gain is only 6% after the fee, and when you factor in average inflation, that 6% becomes 3% real gains, which is nothing to write home about. If, instead, your investment had similar returns but only charged a fee of 0.25%, you would retain most of those gains and still get 7.75%, which nets out to 4.75% after inflation, 58% higher than the 2% fee scenario. 58% is a big deal. And when you compound that 58% year after year, it becomes a huge deal.

The personal finance site NerdWallet did an analysis of the damage fees can do to a younger investor's retirement portfolio, assuming they begin with $25,000 in their retirement accounts at age 25, add $10,000 each year, earn a 7% return in line with long-term, inflation-adjusted averages, and plan to retire in 40 years. If that investor pays a 1% management fee, here's what they stand to lose:

Value Lost to Fees over Time

Number of Years Invested	Portfolio Value Lost to Fees (US Dollars)	After-Fee Investment Value (US Dollars)	Value Lost to Fees (Percent)
10	11,343	166,000	6.4
20	61,696	435,001	12.4
30	210,700	914,215	18.7
40	592,798	1.77 million	25.1

Source: NerdWallet

If that same investor had chosen low-fee index funds instead, they would retire with more than $500,000 additional in their portfolio. A fee of even 1% can do tremendous damage to your gains over time, so program yourself to take a close look at the fees associated with investment options and to aim for well under 1% for every vehicle in which you invest your money, preferably aiming for a tiny fraction of that. Keep both risk and fees in your mind as we walk through the potential investment vehicles you may choose to incorporate into the set of tools that will generate your magic money.

The good news is that it's easier than ever to find high-quality, low-fee investment vehicles and to manage them yourself without having to be an expert.

Investment Vehicles to Consider

Now we'll talk about all of your options for investing your funds to generate magic money that will support you for life, including the pros and cons of each approach and which vehicles are more hands-off versus those that require doing more homework. As we walk through each of your options for investment vehicles, keep in mind that you only need one or two of these to create a solid early retirement financial plan. If you're interested in creating a multifaceted plan with many investment components, that's great, but it's certainly not required. The information here is not intended to make you an expert in any of these investment approaches, but simply to help you make a decision about which vehicles you'd like to incorporate into your tool set and which don't appeal to you. As in every other part of this planning process, play to your strengths. If you want simple above all, there's a great approach here for you. And if you're a spreadsheet whiz who wants to geek out with complexity, lean into that and build a multilayered investing plan. The choice is entirely yours.

Individual Stocks and Bonds

When you talk about investing, most people think about buying individual stocks or bonds. Stocks, also called equities, are tiny slices of companies, and each slice is known as a share. Buying shares makes you a partial owner of that company, and if the company issues dividends to shareholders—the portion of profits left over after paying employees and expenses—you as a partial owner get your share of that money paid out to you periodically.

Bonds, on the other hand, make you a lender. By buying a bond, you are lending money to an entity, usually the federal government or a state or local municipality, with their assurance of paying you back by a certain point, known as the maturity date. Unlike stocks, which can rise and fall in value—what's known as volatility—a bond is sold with a promised future value, known as its yield. That's why bonds are generally thought of as safer than stocks, because their value is guaranteed. However, since the 2008 financial crisis, bond yields have often been lower than the rate of inflation, reintroducing inflationary risk. Despite that risk, most financial experts

still advise keeping a mix of stocks and bonds in your portfolio—
what's called diversification, which we'll discuss in chapter 9—with
the idea that you can sell bonds in periods when stocks are down and
use the stocks to drive your portfolio growth the rest of the time. As
a further benefit, many bonds issued by state and local governments
are tax-free and thus are not subject to capital gains tax, which helps
offset some of their low yield. That said, unless you are in a very
high tax bracket and expect to be there in early retirement as well,
you likely come out ahead avoiding tax-free bonds and purchasing
regularly taxed bonds.

Note, however, that research shows that investors who buy individual stocks do less well historically than the markets as a whole,
capturing only about 80% of the gains made by the markets at large.
That could be explained by two factors: (1) Trading fees on stock
transactions can disproportionately erode gains, especially for investors who trade often, and (2) people who buy individual stocks are
more likely to get caught up in market frenzies and panics, buying
high and selling low, the opposite of the buy-and-hold strategy that
is the cornerstone of creating magic money. Unless you have access to
discounted stock-buying opportunities through an employee stock
purchase plan, avoid making individual stocks a large part of your
portfolio. Bonds, however, are a good hedge against stock market
volatility and belong in your portfolio. If the thought of choosing
which bonds you wish to buy is too daunting to you, bond mutual
funds and index funds (discussed below) are excellent options.

Dividend Stocks

Dividend stocks are a subgroup of stocks in companies that are particularly known for paying out high dividends relative to their share
price, usually in exchange for slower growth, slower asset appreciation, and usually lower volatility. More conservative investors tend

to gravitate toward dividend investing because the strategy provides magic money from dividends without having to sell any shares, which is in some ways the best of both worlds: You get income and you keep all your shares, preserving your capital. The downside of this approach is that dividend stocks tend to appreciate more slowly than growth stocks, providing much smaller gains if and when you do sell them, and under many scenarios, dividend investing will force you to accumulate a larger portfolio than you would need with a drawdown approach, meaning you'll have to work and save longer to generate the necessary magic money cash flow. It also tends to be a more labor-intensive approach to investing because you have to do your homework about which companies' stocks to buy, and you must stay up on financial news to determine if a company you've invested in is likely to see its earnings decrease. So if you prefer to go with as simple an investment approach as possible, dividend investing probably isn't right for you. If you choose to focus on dividend investing, seek out qualified dividend stocks, which have the benefit of lower dividend tax rates if held for more than 60 days.

Mutual Funds and Exchange-Traded Funds (ETFs)

Mutual funds are groupings of stocks or bonds put together by investment managers, usually grouped around a theme, such as large-cap companies (companies with a multibillion-dollar market value) or intermediate-term bonds (bonds that mature in a few years rather than a decade or more). When you buy a share of a mutual fund, you are buying a small slice of all that fund's holdings, and the fund will usually be categorized by its level of risk, ranging from moderate to aggressive, with moderate risk funds likely to see smaller gains but also less risk for big losses, and more aggressive funds having the potential for larger swings in either direction. A fund may also be categorized by whether it is more focused on generating income through higher dividends or on generating more growth in share price by including stocks that are most likely to increase in value. ETFs are nearly identical to mutual funds, but their shares trade on public stock exchanges rather than being available only to customers of a particular investment brokerage firm, and their management fees can be lower than mutual funds.

Most mutual funds and many ETFs are actively managed, meaning that a person or team is analyzing the data available on all publicly traded companies and choosing which stocks and bonds to include in the fund, dumping those that are doing poorly and buying those that they expect to do well. These actively managed funds often tout market-beating returns in the short term, but the companies that offer them are generally less forthcoming about the fact that the high management fees or expense ratios of 1–2% necessary to pay the fund managers a hefty salary erode a large portion of your gains. Because of that, almost no actively managed funds beat or even match the overall market average over the long term.

In addition, because mutual funds generally focus on one asset class, they are usually not well diversified, and it's necessary to own several different mutual funds to manage risk across your portfolio. Some mutual funds known as target date funds manage risk by moving toward more conservative investments as the target date approaches, but these funds have management fees averaging 0.84% according to Morningstar, which is still high enough to erode your gains over the long term.

Index Funds

Stock and bond index funds are a subcategory of mutual funds and ETFs that mirror key stock or bond indices like the S&P 500, the Dow Jones Industrial Average, the total US stock market, or the total US bond market. With index funds, the singular goal is to match the markets, never to beat them. Therefore, index funds are passively managed, and instead of being constantly tweaked to maximize gains, fund managers simply buy shares of the stocks and bonds included in the index they are seeking to mirror, in proportion to the shares in the index, and then sit back and let the magic of compounding happen. That passive management means that investors pay minuscule management fees in relation to actively managed funds, often under 0.25% per year. Some of the broad market index funds with the lowest fees are the Schwab US Broad Market Fund, iShares Core S&P Total US Stock Market Fund, Vanguard Total Stock Market Fund, Fidelity Spartan 500 Index Fund, and a range of other funds with Vanguard, Fidelity, USAA, and T. Rowe Price, all of which have total expense ratios under 0.4%. But even those small percentage differences affect how much magic money you generate from your invested assets, so pay attention to fees even with index funds.

Index funds have other benefits as well, namely in terms of taxes and health care premium calculation. Whenever you or a fund manager sells a share of stock, you trigger what's called a taxable event. The amount that you originally paid for that share is called your cost basis, and the difference between the price for which the share was sold and your cost basis is called your capital gain or capital loss. Capital losses subtract from your taxable income, but capital gains add to it. And your financial plan for the future may involve trying to optimize your income to hit a specific number exactly, both to minimize the income tax you owe and to maximize your health care benefits (more on this in chapter 5). Because index funds aren't actively managed—that is, the fund managers aren't constantly choosing new stocks to include and rebalancing the allocations—there are very few share sales happening behind the scenes that might trigger taxable events that could mess up your careful calculations.

Index funds have grown to become a favorite of savvy investors, now comprising 29% of total invested assets in US markets, with Moody's Investors Service projecting that index funds will surpass half of market holdings by 2024 for all of these reasons.[2] It will probably come as no surprise to know that Mark and I now invest primarily in index funds, and we devote zero brain space to trying to pick the right stocks or mutual funds.

Employer-Sponsored Retirement Accounts: 401(k)s, 403(b)s, 457(b)s, and TSPs

The most commonly used investment tool in the US is the employer-sponsored retirement account, which is generally called a 401(k) at for-profit companies, a 403(b) or 457(b) at nonprofits and state and local governments, and a thrift savings plan (TSP) at federal governmental agencies. But the rules for them are nearly identical, and I'll refer to them collectively as 401(k)s and tax-advantaged retirement plans throughout the book. In any of these plans, an employee can opt to have a certain percentage of their income withheld from a paycheck pretax, meaning before income taxes are calculated on that income (but not before Medicare and Social Security taxes are withheld), and that money is invested according to the employee's elections with an investment brokerage that the employer chooses. Because the money is contributed pretax, you pay income tax on the money only when you take it out of the accounts in retirement, what are known as distributions.

In addition to providing the tax benefit of lowering your taxable income for the year in which you contribute to your 401(k), the primary benefit of employer-sponsored retirement accounts is that employers often offer a match up to some percentage of an employee's contribution. Under the most common scheme, employers match up to 3% of an employee's salary when that employee contributes 6% to the plan. Not taking advantage of that match is quite literally passing up free money as well as a guaranteed return on your investment in the plan. In 2019, the limit on employee contributions to their 401(k) account is $19,000, or $25,000 for those over 50 (it increases every few years), and if you receive an employer match, that total can be even higher.

Some employers offer employees retirement accounts at brokerages that offer a range of low-fee funds, and some do not. But you will generally have a range of investment options available to you within your 401(k), from regular stock mutual funds to target date funds and bond funds. Apply the same skeptical eye toward fees and promised returns to your investment elections within your 401(k) as you would in your own brokerage account.

After you leave work, a question you'll ask yourself is whether to move your funds out of your employer account and into your own individual retirement account (IRA), in what's known as a rollover. The options and management fees involved in your employer plan will dictate whether you want to roll over your assets held there or not. The main restriction on employer-sponsored retirement plans is that you are generally not allowed to withdraw money invested there until you turn 59½ without paying a hefty tax penalty, though there are ways around this that we'll discuss in chapter 6.

Solo 401(k)s

If you are self-employed as a sole proprietor, consultant, or independent contractor, you are eligible to open a solo 401(k), which is similar to an employer-sponsored 401(k) in that you contribute pretax dollars to it and pay income tax on it only when you take distributions in retirement. Also like an employer 401(k), the employee may contribute up to the annual limit ($19,000 in 2019, $25,000 over 50). But unlike a regular 401(k), with a solo 401(k), you as the self-employed person may also make an "employer contribution" of up to 25% of your earned income (not including unearned income like dividends, capital gains, rental income, etc.), so long as your total contributions as both "employee" and "employer" don't exceed $56,000 in 2019 ($62,000 for those over 50).

If you are both traditionally employed and self-employed, you may have both an employer 401(k) and a solo 401(k), but your combined employee contributions to both accounts cannot exceed the current annual limit ($19,000 in 2019, $25,000 over 50).

Individual Retirement Accounts (IRAs)

IRAs are similar to employer-sponsored retirement accounts in that any dollars you contribute are considered pretax and are therefore not included in your taxable income when you calculate how much tax you owe for the year, and you instead pay the taxes when you take distributions in retirement. However, as the name suggests, you manage your IRA individually, and it's up to you to open an account with a brokerage firm that offers low-cost funds that you find desirable. In 2019, IRA contribution limits are $6,000, or $7,000 for those over age 50 under the catch-up provision, though if your modified adjusted gross income is above $64,000 as an individual or $103,000 as a couple, you may only make a partial pretax contribution. Above $74,000 as an individual or $123,000 for a couple, you're ineligible to contribute pretax dollars to an IRA. As with 401(k)s, the contribution limits increase periodically, and income limits also tick upward over time, and as with employer-sponsored plans, there are penalties to withdrawing distributions before you turn 59½, but there are ways around that with IRAs, too, which we'll cover in chapter 6.

Roth IRAs

Roth IRAs are a kind of individual retirement account that function differently in that the dollars you contribute to them are post-tax dollars and do not reduce your income tax in the year you contribute them. However, the benefit is that both your contributions and the gains can be withdrawn tax-free after age 59½, and your contributions can be withdrawn tax-free and penalty-free at any time. Another benefit of Roth IRAs is that they don't carry the same requirement as other retirement accounts of forcing you to begin taking required minimum distributions at age 70½, so if your goal is to pass tax-advantaged money down when you die, Roths are the only vehicle that won't require you to start drawing down your balance in the future, thus leaving that tax-advantaged money in place to pass down. Roth IRA contribution limits for 2018 were the same as for traditional IRAs: $6,000 in 2019, or $7,000 for those over age 50, though the income limits to contribute are significantly higher. If your modified adjusted gross income is above $122,000 as an individual or $193,000 as a couple, you may only make a partial Roth contribution. Above $137,000 as an individual or $203,000 for a couple, you're ineligible to contribute to a Roth IRA directly.

Spousal IRA

If you're in a couple in which one partner does not have an income, you can still open a tax-advantaged account for that person. If you file taxes as married filing jointly, the income-earning spouse can contribute to a spousal IRA for the non-earner, subject to the same maximum contributions and income limits as traditional IRAs, and with the same Roth options, so you can potentially contribute to both a spousal traditional IRA and Roth IRA in a given year. If the stay-at-home partner has some earned income from a home-based business or side gig, he or she can also open an individual or solo 401(k), as discussed above, and contribute up to one-quarter of their earned income, up to a limit of $56,000 per year as of 2019.

Robo Advisors

An increasingly popular way to invest is with a so-called robo advisor, an investment brokerage that uses technological algorithms, rather than highly paid human analysts, to balance and rebalance your portfolio according to your goals (long-term growth, dividends, etc.) and timeline. The promise is that they can get you market-matching or market-beating returns without you having to do a thing other than set up your investment account. They make automatic monthly investing easy and offer high-tech data dashboards with a lot of cool info. Many of these companies promise lower fees than standard mutual fund managers, but the fees are typically still substantially higher than with index funds in which you invest on your own. In addition to having higher fees than many index funds, robo advisors may not always make it obvious when they're changing your investment strategy and charging you more, requiring you to opt out of changes rather than opt in to them. The whole point of using a robo advisor, after all, is to never have to think about your portfolio, so it makes sense that they would not want to bother you with details about changes, though those changes may not always be in your best interest. Another drawback to consider is that with a robo advisor, frequent rebalancing can result in many taxable events being triggered, which could interfere with your tax and health care planning. While the appeal of robo advisors is obvious, setting up an index fund investment strategy is no more difficult and will save you fees.

Health Savings Accounts (HSAs)

Though it's called a savings account, an HSA can be an excellent investment vehicle for early retirement and traditional retirement because it can function as both a savings account and an investment account in which you allocate funds to the investment vehicles of your choice based on what your account provider offers. The Affordable Care Act (ACA) includes a provision that allows employers to offer high-deductible health plans and allows individuals to buy similar plans on the health care exchanges that then allow the individual to open an HSA, a portable investment account that allows individuals to save for large health care expenses. An HSA can have significant tax benefits, but it is not without some major drawbacks. On the benefits side, HSAs are the rare investment vehicle that are triple tax advantaged: Dollars contributed to the accounts are either tax-deductible if saved by an individual or pretax if deducted from an employee's payroll, the interest earned on the account will never be taxed, and account holders can withdraw money tax-free to pay for qualified medical expenses. Because you can keep your HSA even after you change jobs, and in theory keep it forever, it sounds like the perfect way to save for health care expenses later in life. However, the major downside is that in order to qualify for an HSA, you must be enrolled in a high-deductible health plan, meaning that your insurance company won't pay a cent of your health care costs until you hit your deductible, an amount that commonly tops $10,000 a year for family plans. If potentially paying $10,000 out of pocket before your insurance kicks in and an additional copay on expenses beyond that doesn't sound appealing, then an HSA is probably not a good option for you.

Analysis shows that most people will come out ahead sticking with more traditional, moderate-deductible health insurance, assuming you have a choice of plans. Those for whom HSAs might be a good option for a few years are folks who are young and healthy, with enough cash flow to pay medical costs like copays and deductibles out-of-pocket, and with jobs in which employers are contributing at least $1,000 a year to your HSA for you. But for everyone else, economic research suggests that the tax benefits of HSAs are more than offset by higher medical costs in the meantime, as well as the care that many people simply opt not to get. Commonwealth Fund research shows that people on high-deductible plans skimp on necessary care because the cost barrier is too high. And even worse, data show that a full third of people on high-deductible plans don't even get their *free* preventive services mandated by the ACA due to the mental barrier of those high deductibles. Your health is too important to sacrifice for a small tax benefit, so think carefully before opting for a high-deductible plan just because it offers an HSA.

Of course, if a high-deductible plan with an HSA is the only thing your employer offers, by all means take it. And then use the HSA to your advantage if you can—and don't neglect your preventive care.

Rental Real Estate

Investing in rental real estate—whether that's condos, apartment buildings, or single-family homes—can be one of the fastest routes to a work-optional life because you need far less cash saved to generate enough magic money or passive income to live off of. The flip side, of course, is that that's made possible by leverage, a fancy word for debt. Most real estate investors take out a mortgage on a property they wish to buy to rent it out. They do the math on the purchase price and local rental market to ensure that the rent they collect will cover the mortgage payments, taxes, insurance, income tax they'll owe, and upkeep costs and still net some magic money at the end, what's often called positive cash flow. To be a successful rental real estate investor, you have to be comfortable being in debt for the long term, perhaps deeply in debt if you have multiple properties, and you have to be willing to do the legwork to get to know the local market where you'll be investing. It also helps to be handy so that you don't have to outsource every repair, and to enjoy being a landlord, but those aren't mandatory.

In addition to being able to achieve a work-optional life relatively quickly through rental real estate (relative to building up enough stock and bond assets to support you forever) there are other benefits like not having to buy properties only where you live, so you can invest in a market where conditions are more favorable to landlords (for example, with lower purchase prices and higher rents), and not having to manage the property yourself if you're willing to give some of your revenue to a property manager to do the day-to-day work for you. The downsides, in addition to debt that may not feel comfortable to everyone, are that you can't liquidate property assets quickly should you need to free up cash, you take on the challenge of dealing with tenants who may or may not respect your property or pay rent on time, you absorb the cost of inevitable vacancies between tenants, and you tie much of your livelihood to the health of the local economy where you're invested rather than the more diversified national and world economies. If you sell the property one day without having lived in it for at least two years of the last five, you'll owe capital gains tax on every penny of its increase in value.

If you decide that rental real estate is an appealing path for you, the good news is that it isn't all or nothing. You can purchase a single rental property, like we did, or if you move, you can keep your former home to use as a rental if the math works out to make it favorable, hiring a property manager if necessary in exchange for a fixed percentage of the rent collected. Professional property investors often use a ratio called the capitalization rate or cap rate to determine if a property would be a good rental, calculated by dividing the net annual income (subtracting from the rent you collect all expenses like maintenance, insurance, and taxes, but not including mortgage payments) by the property's purchase price. Investors typically consider a 4% cap rate acceptable in a high-demand area in which vacancy is expected to be low, but usually aim to get closer to 10% or even more. For example, if you buy a rental property for $250,000, you want to clear at least $10,000 annually after expenses. When making this calculation, it's essential to be realistic about what rent a property could collect and what the associated expenses would total. It's also a good idea to follow the 1% rule, which says that the rent you collect each month should total at least 1% of your total principal investment (the purchase price plus any improvements). And far too many new real estate investors forget to factor in income tax. If you are also employed, every penny of new rental income will be taxed at your highest marginal rate, and that tax can easily make the difference between a property that's cash flow positive and cash flow negative, aka a money pit. All of that said, if the risks involved with rental real estate don't scare you, and you're willing to do your homework to sniff out the good values in the area where you're looking to invest, rentals can absolutely be the fastest path to a work-optional life, and this route is certainly worth considering.

Chad Carson began his career in his early 20s as an entrepreneur with only $1,000 to his name. He found that the constant hustle was wearing on him, making him question whether he'd ever earn enough to provide for the family he hoped to have one day or be able to stop worrying about money constantly. He stumbled upon the concept of rental real estate investing and decided that that was the path to financial independence that was most interesting to him. By saving up enough to make the down payment on a low-cost property, often a modest multifamily apartment building or basic single-family home, and then using the cash flow from the rent he collected to save for the next property, he quickly built up a portfolio of dozens of units by his early 30s that now provide enough income to cover all the expenses for him, his wife, and their two children. They live a modest lifestyle and don't need much to cover their expenses. And they're comfortable with the mortgage debt because they saved cash reserves and only bought properties that had a significant cushion between the rental income and the mortgage and maintenance costs, so they can weather extended vacancies without concern. Chad and his family recently spent a year in Ecuador and plan to continue traveling with their newfound financial freedom.

Real Estate Investment Trusts (REITs)

If you like the idea of profiting off rental real estate, but you don't want to take on all the risk yourself—or do all the work of managing properties—another option is to invest in real estate investment trusts. REITs are investment companies that serve as the manager for real estate on behalf of their investors, usually managing large-scale rental properties like apartments, shopping centers, or office buildings. Investors receive dividends based on the companies' profits. You can buy shares of REITs on the major stock exchanges or by purchasing shares in real estate mutual funds that invest in multiple REITs. As with any investment, it's important to do your homework to ensure that you aren't paying overly high management fees and that the REIT you're buying isn't invested in tanking assets, like shopping malls whose tenants are all moving out in an age of dying retail.

Pensions

Though not something you invest in, a pension may still be part of your magic money tool set if you're one of the lucky few who still has a defined-benefit pension. If so, you have a leg up on being able to retire early. Most pensions are linked to length of service, not age, and therefore you may be able to qualify for benefits in as little as 20 years, which could be in your 40s or 50s. That said, a great many government and private sector pensions have been scaled back in recent years as health and benefits costs for retirees have climbed faster than inflation, and so you should consider a pension one tool in your magic money tool set, not the only tool. Make sure you have other magic money–generating vehicles working for you so that you don't wake up one day to discover your pension has been cut and you have no other options.

Delnora Loyd and her husband, Wes, met in the army in their early 20s and now have three young children. While Wes has since left the army for the private sector, Delnora remains in service as a physician with a specialty in treating cancer. Though she earns less than she could in private practice, she'll be eligible for a retired military pension and health care benefits in her mid-40s, which will allow both of them to retire at that time. Because she loves her work and derives great meaning from it, Delnora expects to continue working a few stints a year as a *locum tenens* physician after she retires from the army, filling in for other doctors out on leave, but when and how often she does so will be entirely on her own terms. And their whole family will have plenty of time home together while the kids are still young.

Social Security

Social Security is an incredibly complex subject often consuming entire books, but because it is likely to be a source of at least some magic money for you in your traditional retirement years, it's worth discussing here. Social Security is similar to a defined-benefit plan run by the government to ensure that everyone has a basic level of income in their later years. The government withholds a certain amount of your income throughout your working years, and the more you pay in, the more you get back, up to a fairly modest limit. And though there will always be those warning that the Social Security trust fund is on the verge of financial ruin, for most people working today, there's very little chance that you'll get nothing paid out to you from Social Security.

Here are a few key facts to remember about Social Security: For everyone born after 1960, "full retirement age" is considered 67. You can claim benefits as early as age 62, but your benefits will be greatly reduced. And for every year you wait to claim Social Security benefits, your payout amount increases by 8%, which is one of the biggest guaranteed returns you can get anywhere, making it in most people's interest to put off claiming benefits as long as possible, living instead off your other sources of magic money in your early and mid-60s.

How much you receive in your Social Security check is calculated by averaging your highest 35 earning years, and the statements you receive from the Social Security Administration that project your expected benefit base this number on the assumption that you will work continuously until at least age 62 if not age 67. This makes it especially tricky for early retirees or semiretirees to calculate how much you may one day receive, because there could be many zero-income years included in that average.

If you're considering an extremely early retirement, say in your late 20s or early 30s, keep in mind that to qualify at all to receive Social Security, you must have accumulated 40 credits, which for most salaried employees works out to 10 years of full-time work, whether that's traditional or self-employment. Retiring too early may mean not having enough credits accumulated and disqualifying yourself from receiving Social Security benefits one day. And even though you'll have earnings in retirement from your magic money sources, most of that does not count as earned income, and thus does not earn you Social Security credits. Unearned income that doesn't increase your Social Security benefits includes capital gains, rental income, interest on savings, IRA or 401(k) withdrawals, private pensions, payouts for vacation or sick leave, bonuses, and deferred compensation. In other words, just about every possible passive income source.

Though it's possible that Social Security benefits could decrease, especially for higher earners, to keep the system solvent longer, it's helpful to know the ballpark ranges you might be looking at. While there is no minimum benefit, and those who have paid very little into the system will receive very little in return, the average monthly benefit for someone who reached full retirement age in 2016 was $1,340, while the maximum benefit for the highest earners was $2,640, a total of less than $32,000 per year before taxes. In most parts of the country that's not enough to live on, especially when you consider the costs that come with Medicare (more on this in chapter 5), so Social Security should not be your primary source of income in any part of your retirement. If you wish to be extra cautious, you can even leave Social Security out of your calculations—as we do—and consider it gravy when you get it one day, or you could include, say, half of the current average benefit in your assumptions, depending on how many years you expect to pay into the Social Security system.

529 College Savings Funds

It may seem odd to include a college savings fund in a list of investment vehicles for early retirement, but if you're a parent or caregiver planning to pay for a child's college in the future, then saving for that purpose will be an important component of your work-optional financial plan. These 529 plans are tax-advantaged, state-sponsored tuition savings plans. If you intend to pay for part or all of the college education for yourself or someone you love, investing in a 529 college savings plan may make sense, though not necessarily. Much like an HSA or a Roth IRA, the money inside a 529 plan compounds tax-free and may be withdrawn tax-free to pay for qualified higher educational expenses such as tuition, room and board, and books, as well as for graduate school expenses. Whether a 529 makes sense for you has much to do with what state you live in. Most states do not give savers a choice in how the money is invested, and some state plans come with unacceptably high management fees that offset a large part of the tax benefit. Some states allow a tax deduction for contributions to a 529 while others don't, though it's never a federal tax deduction. In addition, if your children decide not to go to college, the only way to get the money back is to pay taxes on the gains along with a 10% penalty. Finally, when financial aid is calculated, 529 funds count as parental nonretirement assets and may be assumed to be allocated entirely for an older child when in fact intended to benefit multiple children and may result in less financial aid than you would have gotten if you'd instead saved those funds in your own retirement accounts. This may force you to exhaust the funds on the first child to go to college, having little left for children that follow. If you don't expect to qualify for financial aid and feel confident that your child or children will go to college, 529 plans can make a great deal of sense, so long as you aren't in a state with overly restrictive or high-fee plans.

Passive Business Ventures

If you have a naturally creative or entrepreneurial streak, you may be drawn to create a magic money stream out of a business that you build on your own. The only limit here is your own imagination, but the ideal passive business venture is one that requires very little effort from you to manage—otherwise it's just another job, even if you work for yourself! A friend of ours has created a great example of a passive business venture that supports a good portion of his lifestyle without him having to do much. He built an online business that sells custom hacky sacks, and other than selecting a factory and getting the whole venture up and running, his only real ongoing task is to check in periodically that the website stays functional and that orders are being fulfilled as promised. But most of the "work" happens elsewhere—the factory he contracts with receives the orders, manufactures the products, and ships them to buyers. He collects mostly passive income just for having had the idea and for doing the startup work, and there's no reason to think he won't have this magic money coming in for years to come.

Ideal passive business ventures require little of your time once you get past the initial setup, either because you can outsource the labor to an entity that doesn't require direct management or because you create a tool that customers can use without your input required, such as building a piece of software people can purchase or use online. Another option is to build a business that can be sold, with the proceeds then funding your other magic money vehicles.

Savings Vehicles to Supplement Your Investments

Every work-optional plan should include a cash cushion for money you may need in the short or intermediate term, for example, your emergency fund, money you're saving for a down payment on a home, and eventually your retirement cash cushion. All of the investment vehicles above have the potential to grow significantly faster than the rate of inflation, meaning that when you invest in them, your spending power will increase over time. That's what you want in your magic money or passive income–generating portfolio. However, it's also important to use the right vehicles for cash savings so that you won't need to sell stocks or trigger taxable events to access funds, something you won't want to do if the markets are down at that moment. The savings vehicles you should consider having in your tool set include:

High-Interest Savings Accounts

High-interest savings accounts, most often offered by online-only banks, pay a better interest rate than do regular savings accounts at most banks, and they have the benefit of being FDIC insured. Open a high-interest savings account at a bank other than your primary one to make it a little harder to access this money, and park your emergency fund here. The more hurdles there are to getting your hands on this pool of funds, the less likely you are to spend the money for a purpose other than the intended one. Aim to save at least $2,000 in this account initially, and work up to three to six months of essential expenses. Eventually, as you get close to early retirement, you'll also build up this account to include two to three years' worth of expenses in cash, to buffer against having to sell shares when the markets are down significantly. And if you're saving for a rental real estate purchase, a high-interest savings account is a good place to park both the down payments you're saving and your cash buffer. Avoid investing money you'll need in the next few years in stocks and keep it in cash instead.

"Life Happens" Savings Account

Suze Orman coined this term for a savings account geared toward covering unexpected expenses that don't quite rise to the level of emergency. Consider opening this savings account at your regular bank, and work toward keeping a few thousand dollars here in addition to the full amount you save in your emergency fund off-site at another bank. Then, if you need an unexpected car repair or must fly last-minute to a funeral, you'll have funds available that won't sink your budget or deplete your emergency fund. An added benefit to this account is that it keeps you in the habit of not tapping into your emergency fund and thinking of it as untouchable except in true emergencies, like losing your job, needing expensive medical care, or having your home destroyed in a natural disaster.

Donor-Advised Fund (DAF)

If donating to charitable causes is important to you and something you wish to continue doing in retirement even when you're earning less, consider opening a donor-advised fund. A DAF is like a cross between a brokerage account and your own mini philanthropic foundation. You make a contribution to your DAF and receive the charitable tax deduction in the year of your contribution, but then have control over those funds to grant out to charitable organizations of your choice over however many years you wish to stretch them. From a tax perspective, you donated the money when you put it into the DAF, and while you can't get the money back, you retain control over how it's invested and who receives it. Since the 2017 tax reform law raised the standard deduction on tax returns, the bar is now higher to be able to claim itemized deductions, which charitable contributions fall under. So you might decide to batch your contributions to a DAF, that is, claim the standard deduction most years, but save up enough to itemize a larger charitable contribution to your DAF once every two or three years. You can repeat this cycle with new DAF contributions, and then use the funds already in your DAF to continue giving charitably even in years when you aren't making "new" charitable contributions for tax purposes. You may also aim, as we did, to make a large contribution to your DAF after you've hit your retirement goal magic number but before you stop working so that you get a large tax deduction in your last working year, when you're likely to be in your highest tax bracket. The DAF will then allow you to continue to make charitable donations over a long period in retirement without dipping into your magic money to do so. This is a great way to focus on philanthropy all throughout your lifetime. The lowest-fee DAF options, which also have the lowest initial contribution requirements, are with Fidelity and Charles Schwab, though a number of other institutions like Vanguard also offer them.

Vehicles to Leave Out of Your Magic Money Tool Set

There are other potential ways to save as well, some of which financial experts will tell you are essential or are good investments, but which may straight up be bad investments and have no place in your tool set. Two vehicles that investment advisors who work on commission love to recommend are annuities and cash value life insurance. They do so because they receive a large kickback from selling these products, not because these are great investment vehicles for consumers.

Annuities

Annuities are contracts purchased from an insurance company guaranteeing a certain monthly payout in exchange for a set amount that you invest. Many people are drawn to the certainty that some annuities offer, for example, by promising a fixed payout regardless of what the markets are doing, but that certainty comes at a cost. Most annuities involve huge management fees that eat into your gains significantly, and because the payout amount is set, the insurance company, and not you, gets the benefit of larger market gains. Most financial experts recommend against annuities except as a penalty-free way to access IRA funds before age 59½, but there are better, more cost-effective ways to access those funds.

Cash Value Life Insurance

Cash value life insurance, often called whole life or universal life, is popular among insurance brokers and commission-based financial advisors because it offers an especially large kickback to them, and it appeals to many consumers because it provides a guaranteed cash value that can be withdrawn or borrowed against. However, over the life of the policy, most policyholders will typically pay in much more than the policy is worth, and much *much* more than the policy's cash value, because the management fees on these policies are so high. To put this in perspective, to get a comparable amount of life insurance coverage, you'll typically pay eight times as much for cash value life insurance as you will for equivalent term life insurance. You'll come out much farther ahead buying a term life policy (more on this in chapter 9) and investing the difference in your magic money port-folio. If you've already bought a whole life or universal life policy, consider taking out the cash value you've accumulated, moving that money into a higher-yield investment, and canceling the policy.

The Best Approach to Investing: Aim for Simple and Hands-Off

Now that we've talked through all the possible investment vehicles that you can use to fund your work-optional life, you can begin to reflect on which feel like they suit you best. You may want to invest only in index funds in both your 401(k) at work and your additional taxable investments. You might enjoy the idea of finding homes, fix-ing them up, and managing them as rental properties, and go all in on rental real estate. Or you may go for some combination plan like some index fund investments, some dividend stocks, a single rental property, a 529 for your kids' college, and a health savings account for future health care expenses. As in all of this, there's no right or wrong answer, and it's up to you to think about which options you gravitate toward. Then, you can set your investments up in the simplest way possible so that you don't need to think too much about them and don't even have to worry about how the stock markets are doing.

It's for good reason that index funds are continually growing in popularity, because they provide automatically diversified investments with the lowest possible fees, therefore keeping your returns consistently in line with the markets as a whole and avoiding the erosion of returns to fees that happens with actively managed funds. More exciting approaches to investing, like day trading or picking individual stocks, will make you feel compelled to check in on your accounts too often, which may spur you to do something emotional, like sell shares when the markets are diving or buy shares when the markets are skyrocketing. If you want the simplest, easiest investing approach possible, go with index funds.

Ideally, you'll invest automatically and regularly in your chosen vehicles, either monthly or twice each month. Your goal is to invest for the long term, investing on schedule no matter what the markets are doing, and then keeping your hands off of it until you begin living off your magic money sources. As to where you invest it, that's up to you, but choosing one or two diversified stock funds and one or two diversified bond funds will keep you well covered. Some favorites of financial experts and early retirees are the Vanguard Total Stock Market Index Fund (VTSMX or VTSAX) and Total Bond Market Index Fund (VBMFX or VBTLX), S&P 500 index funds like the Fidelity Spartan 500 fund, and other index funds with extremely low fees. Because these funds already invest in a broad swath of the stock and bond markets, you don't have to worry about choosing the right mix of assets to insulate you from risk and expose you to growth opportunities. You get a mix of everything: large and small companies, stocks that have the potential to sustain significant growth over time, stocks that generate large dividends, and the real estate holdings of the companies whose stock you own.

If you already have an account with a large brokerage firm that offers low-fee index funds, all you'll need to do is set up automated monthly or twice-monthly investments into the stock and bond index funds of your choice. If you don't already have a brokerage account, choose a financial institution like Vanguard, Fidelity, USAA, Charles Schwab, or T. Rowe Price that offers a broad range of low-fee index funds and has minimum investment requirements in line with your current situation. For example, Vanguard, a favorite of DIY investors for its low fees, requires a minimum investment of $3,000 for most of its mutual funds and charges a higher management fee until your balance in any given index fund tops $10,000, which they call going from investor shares to admiral shares. If you are just beginning to invest, you may not have that much capital handy and thus may elect to start out with an institution like Charles Schwab, which will allow you to invest in index funds with its automatic investment program for as little as $100 a month. If you're eligible for USAA membership, they offer a similar program and allow you to begin investing in a select group of starter funds for $50 or more each month. After you've built up enough in your account to meet the minimum for other brokerages, you can investigate whether it's worth moving your investment to another institution with lower fees.

If rental real estate appeals most to you as your vehicle to early retirement, please consult this book's "Additional Resources" section. Real estate investing is a much more specialized approach to investing, with many more factors to consider. Fortunately, there are great resources out there to help you get started.

INVESTMENT CHECKLIST

☐ Investigate what investment options you have through your and/or a spouse's employer(s), such as 401(k), 403(b), 457(b), TSP, and employee stock purchase plan.

☐ Ensure that you're saving as much in your employer plan as you can comfortably afford, preferably enough to get the full employer match if you have that benefit.

☐ Assign employer plan contributions to the stock and bond fund options with the lowest fees.

☐ Determine which investment vehicles you'd like to focus on outside of your employer plan, whether that's low-fee index funds, actively managed mutual funds, individual stocks and bonds, dividend stocks, rental real estate, passive business ventures, or some combination.

☐ Choose a primary brokerage firm and set up automated investing.

☐ Open new savings accounts as needed.

CHAPTER 5

Plan Permanently for the Biggest Comforts: Shelter and Health Care

Good health is not something we can buy. However, it can be an extremely valuable savings account.

—ANNE WILSON SCHAEF

Though getting started with planning for a work-optional life can feel daunting at first, the good news is that peace of mind follows quickly behind when you realize that you've taken control of your financial future. You're now on the road to permanent financial security, and that's hugely empowering. Especially after you know that you're set for life on two of the biggest necessities—housing and health care—you'll relieve any lingering financial anxiety you may feel, something most people never experience.

Keeping a Roof over Your Head

When thinking about housing, you have the opportunity to dream. If you could live anywhere in the world without worrying about whether you could find a job there, where would it be? We'll take your reflections on this question from chapter 2 and expand on them here, imagining all the possibilities of the conventional and unconventional ways you can keep a roof over your head. Just as with creating your cache of magic money, you have lots of options about how to provide shelter for yourself throughout your life—and how you do that may very well change in each phase of life. Most of us are renters when we first start working, a subset go on to own a home (or two or three or more over time), and many people downsize to smaller accommodations later in life.

Those working toward an unconventional, work-optional life may choose to broaden this set of options even more, thinking not just about the question of whether to rent or to own a home but whether to be stationary at all. An increasing number of early retirees are choosing to retire on the road, either living full-time in a recreational vehicle (RV) or embarking on a life of full-time travel, paying for hotels and Airbnb rooms instead of paying rent or a mortgage.

There's no right or wrong answer here, but I recommend you make sure to build enough financial wiggle room into your plan that you can change your mind if you so choose. If you quit your job to hit the road as a full-time RVer and decide a year later that you are ready to live in a house again, you'll be much happier if you have magic money streams coming in to afford to pay rent somewhere rather than being forced to stick it out. And beyond just changing your mind, living in a tiny house with your bed up a ladder full-time may not work so well if you become sick or disabled in your later years. A well-developed housing vision has a plan for now and the flexibility to create a new plan should you find yourself with different interests or with more limited mobility later on.

In part I we talked about where you see yourself living in your work-optional life, so let's go back to that part of your life vision. Is that place you envision where you live now or someplace different? If it's where you live now, is it in your current home, or in a different one, maybe a smaller one? Cutting down on housing expenses is one of the fastest, most effective ways to save money, so you might choose to downsize your living arrangements now, well in advance of achieving your work-optional life, to speed your progress. Or perhaps your dream home isn't one place at all but instead a nomadic life of constant travel.

Let's talk first about options if your goal is to have a stationary home base, as it always has been for Mark and me. We love to travel and to camp, but we also love knowing that we have a home to return to where things are just as we left them. And while we may not stay in Tahoe forever, we feel lucky to get to live here for now, and we feel no need to maintain the flexibility that renting would give us. Owning a home feels like the right decision for us, but that doesn't make it the right choice for everyone.

For decades, the conventional wisdom has been that it's better to own a home than to rent. And renting has been described as "throwing money away." That's not even remotely true, however. Owning a home comes with a great many costs the owner never recoups, and it locks up capital for the long term that can't easily be accessed. It also takes many years of paying off a mortgage before most buyers will accrue significant equity in their home. And 2018 data show that, in nearly half of all US counties, it's cheaper in the long term to rent than buy: 64% of the US population lives where it's more affordable to rent than to buy.[1] That could change, of course, as we saw after the 2008 financial crisis, when buying became cheaper than renting for a few years, but the old conventional wisdom that buying is always better is worth examining.

The question of whether to rent or buy is also a highly personal one, not a simple math problem, with a number of variables such as what your local market dynamics are, which arrangement feels better to you, how attached you want to be to one place, how important it is to you to customize your space, and whether you want to tie up resources to save for a down payment rather than saving for another goal (like early retirement). Let's go over the pros and cons of each option.

When you own a home, assuming you finance it with a fixed-rate mortgage that has either a 15-year or a 30-year term, you have certainty about how much your payment will be over the long term. You may still have increases in your property taxes, insurance, and utility payments, but you'll never be surprised. If you stay in your home long enough, you may also one day pay off your mortgage and have no mortgage payment, which allows you to live quite cheaply. And if property prices increase while you're living in your home and you decide to sell, you get to keep that extra money, which is why ardent proponents of home ownership will refer to your home as "an investment." Though recent tax law changes have capped how much you can write off on your federal income tax return of your mortgage interest and state and local property taxes, there's still a tax benefit to owning as well, though how big a benefit that is for you will vary based on your income and tax rates. There's also a big emotional aspect to owning a home: knowing you can customize it as you wish and that no one can kick you out so long as you pay your mortgage and property taxes. On the negative side, you must deal with all repairs yourself, either doing the work or paying someone else to do it. Most people underestimate the costs of home ownership and are surprised by how much money they must pour into repairs, especially in the first few years of owning. And you may find yourself unable to move when you wish to if you aren't able to sell your house at a fair price.

On the other hand, when you rent, you aren't building equity, you often can't make changes to the property, and you benefit from no tax write-offs. Your rent can also go up unexpectedly, depending on local rent control rules. But for the majority of people, you'll spend less money renting than buying, you won't lock up huge sums of money in your investment, and you don't have to deal with repairs yourself. And research shows that if you're disciplined about investing the money you would be spending to buy in your market versus what it costs to rent, you can come out ahead of those who do buy their homes, because the stock markets tend to give better long-term returns than the housing market. Of course, that's a big *if*, dependent on how the markets do over the period and whether you actually invest the money you're not paying to a mortgage instead of spending it.

The choice of whether to rent or buy can seem especially complicated, but given the pros and cons of each, make sure your gut gets a say in the matter. One or the other will feel better to you, and that's valid. Often it comes down to the question of which you value more: certainty of how much your housing will cost or flexibility to keep your assets liquid and to move whenever you want.

If you do decide to buy a home, the next decision will be whether to pay off your mortgage early, especially before you reach early retirement. The less you spend on your home, the more of your income you can devote to other savings goals, and if you choose a modest home instead of the biggest, most expensive home the banks say you can afford, paying it off ahead of schedule may be a viable option for you. But should you do it?

Mark and I bought our house in Tahoe in 2011, near the bottom of the real estate market following the 2008 financial crisis. Despite the banks telling us that they'd happily lend us much more than we wanted to borrow, we stuck to our budget, bought a house priced well below the median, and financed it on a 15-year mortgage. Not that we weren't tempted by nicer houses. It's so easy to fall into thinking, *Well, it's only $200 more a month...* But ultimately our decision to buy less house than the banks would have lent us was driven not by financial savviness but by fear. We were scarred by the 2008 financial crisis and saw friends lose homes, destroy their credit with short sales, and struggle to find steady work for years after being laid off. Because of that, we were determined to keep our mortgage payment small enough that we could still handle the payments along with other necessities if we had to do so on one income.

At that point, we were still calling our pie-in-the-sky early retirement idea our 10-year plan, so we decided that we'd try to pay off the mortgage in 10 years. But as it became clear that we could probably retire sooner than 10 years from our start date, we had a decision to make: Should we pay off the house even earlier or invest more so that we could cover the mortgage payments until it was paid off? There are solid arguments on both sides: The "don't pay it off early" camp will remind you that the markets historically return well above the mortgage interest rates in the 3-4% range that we were seeing in the 2010s. To them, not paying it off is a no-brainer, because you're trading away higher possible returns for the comfort of knowing that your home is paid off. The "do pay it off early" camp will stress one word: *possible*. It's also possible that markets won't return average rates during the key years, and that you'll actually come out ahead paying your mortgage off early. Regardless, they'll say that paying your mortgage off early gives you a guaranteed return of whatever your interest rate is, which is likely to be higher than any other guaranteed rate of return out there.

But for us, it honestly came down to emotions. I'm definitely on the risk-averse end of the financial spectrum, and the thought of owning our home outright and knowing that no matter how badly we mismanaged our finances, we'd still have a roof over our head let me sleep well at night. With a paid-off house, we can live incredibly cheaply if the markets tank or stay stagnant for a long period, which gives our early retirement financial plan extra security. For us, it was an easy answer, but as always, that might not be the right choice for you. And it might not even be the right choice for us permanently. If we decide in our later years that we're sick of the cold winters and move to a lower-elevation area, there's a good chance that we'd go back to being renters at that point, instead of buying another home, so that we aren't on the hook for the maintenance work or the accompanying costs. So what's right for you now doesn't have to be what's right for you forever.

Speaking of forever, there's one more consideration to keep in mind when planning your housing: The housing arrangement that suits you now may not work especially well if your circumstances change. We'll talk about health care in the next section, but one fact that's relevant for housing is that Medicare, the federal health insurance program for people over 65, has limited coverage for skilled nursing care, meaning that you'll have enormous out-of-pocket costs should you need to move into a nursing home or spend an extended stay in a rehabilitation facility. But Medicare has good coverage for in-home health care, requiring minimum out-of-pocket expenditures to get similar skilled nursing care at home. It's a compelling argument for ensuring that you give yourself the financial flexibility to spend your later years in a home where you can age in place and, for example, where you can make modifications if necessary like making the home wheelchair-friendly. So if you decide to spend your early retirement in an RV or a tiny house, build in a plan and funding to go along with it to move into a more stationary arrangement should you one day require it.

Maintaining Access to Quality Health Care

If you don't already see your health as one of your most important assets, change your mindset right this second. There's a good chance that the work-optional life you've envisioned for yourself relies on some expectation of being able to enjoy your life and being able-bodied enough to do things you aspire to do outside of work. And while life spans on the whole are increasing, quality years of life are actually decreasing, a troubling trend to anyone hoping to live a long, healthy, fun retirement. Enjoying good health for many years to come requires not only making an effort in your personal life to eat healthily and get plenty of physical activity, but it also relies on having continuous access to excellent health care, something that's not automatic in the US. Fortunately, living a work-optional life can come with less stress and more time for exercise and healthy cooking, all things that increase your chances of staying in vibrant health for a long time. And, there are now better options than there were only a few years ago for early retirees and those without health insurance through work to buy coverage.

The US is one of the only wealthy nations in the world that has historically tied health care coverage to employment. It's an odd arrangement, to have our employers dictate to us what plans we can choose from and how much they cost, but it's the system we have. And until recently, this system made early retirement and all forms of work-optional living much more challenging than they are now, because people younger than Medicare-qualification age (65) had few options for obtaining health insurance on their own.

That all changed with the passage of the Affordable Care Act (ACA) in 2010, also known as Obamacare. In addition to creating an individual marketplace that allows people to buy plans directly from insurers instead of having to go through an employer or expensive insurance broker, the ACA also made most types of preventive care entirely free, it allowed kids to stay on their parents' insurance until age 26, and it outlawed old practices of denying coverage for preexisting conditions. While the ACA has been hotly contested politically since its passage, most health care experts believe it is here to stay in some form, which is good news for early retirees, as we do not have to worry about being unable to secure health insurance in the absence of traditional employment.

Mark and I both have preexisting conditions—his autoimmune

and mine genetic—and knowing that we can buy insurance and get the care we need thanks to the ACA is one of the main reasons we felt comfortable actually pulling the ripcord to early retirement. If there was no ACA, we would still have just as much saved, but might very well be stuck working forever just for the assurance of keeping access to health insurance. Fortunately, there is no longer a barrier between early retirement and health insurance, so nothing to stop you from making the leap to retirement after you've hit your financial targets.

As with the other choices you'll make in your work-optional plan—especially around magic money and housing—you have options with health care, and they change over the course of your lifetime. Whichever options you choose, I urge you to see them as essential, not optional. While the idea of covering preexisting conditions is incredibly popular with voters, the rules around coverage of them could still change any time, and past rules could go back into effect that allowed insurers to deny coverage of preexisting conditions to those who'd had a gap in their coverage. In addition, despite the ACA getting more people insured than ever before, medical bills are still the leading cause of bankruptcy, including for people with health insurance. Make continuous, comprehensive health insurance coverage a nonnegotiable cornerstone of your financial plan.

COBRA

If you had health insurance through an employer, that employer is required by law to offer you COBRA insurance for 18 months. COBRA coverage is identical to the insurance you had through work, but without your employer subsidizing any part of the coverage, meaning that it is usually quite expensive. On average, employer plans cover 82% of medical costs, a high level of coverage relative to other plans available, and if you opt to go on COBRA after leaving the job, you'll be on the hook for the full bill for this potentially cushy coverage. Before electing to accept COBRA coverage, price out your options on the health care exchange plans available to you, knowing that the exchange plans will likely end up being cheaper.

Exchange Plans

Since the passage of the ACA, exchange plans have been available in every state in the US, either through the federal Healthcare.gov exchange or through individual state exchanges. Exchange plans, often called Obamacare plans, are just like regular private health insurance, though with a few notable features. To help consumers compare plans, ACA plans are grouped by levels, with bronze plans covering 60% of expenses, silver plans covering 70%, gold covering 80%, and platinum covering 90%. Most people who purchase exchange insurance policies opt for silver-level plans that cover 70% of medical costs, and if your prior employer plan was typical and covered 82% of costs, you may notice more out-of-pocket costs after transitioning to an ACA plan. In addition, to save costs, ACA plans typically have 40% fewer specialists in their networks, and many primary care physicians listed are not currently accepting new patients. So it's essential to do your homework ahead of enrolling to ensure that your doctors are in network for the new plan you choose. When Mark and I went from work insurance to ACA insurance, we switched from the Blue Cross Blue Shield network at work to the same network on an exchange plan and assumed all of our doctors would still be covered. Wrong. Our new plan had fewer providers to choose from and had higher copays for everything, higher drug costs, and a higher deductible. We're still grateful to have the coverage available to us, but it was a rude awakening. If you'll be relying on health coverage through the exchange, get used to the idea that you'll need to shop carefully for your policy each and every year during the open enrollment period, and to check for provider network changes, changes to copays and deductibles, and—most important of all—changes to the out-of-pocket maximum. The ACA mandates that all plans must have a stated out-of-pocket maximum, after which they must cover all of your medical costs, and this number is like your worst-case scenario. When shopping for plans, the out-of-pocket max should be the most important factor you consider, because you may end up on the hook for that amount if you or someone in your family gets sick or has an accident. If paying the full max amount would sink your budget for that year, consider a plan that costs a bit more each month but gives you a smaller out-of-pocket maximum.

The second big aspect of ACA plans that is helpful to early retirees is that they truly are the closest thing to "affordable" coverage that we have. ACA plan premiums are going up each year, but at a much slower rate than non-exchange plans, which is a positive for everyone relying on the exchanges. And, the premium you pay is tied to your income, which for many early retirees is low (as opposed to basing premiums on your assets, which are likely to be high). While this fact agitates quite a few people who disapprove of high-net-worth people receiving subsidies to help pay for their health insurance, neither party has signaled any interest in changing that particular part of the law. And the US has a long history of adopting programs that adjust only on basis of income, not on assets, what's known as means testing, not asset testing. So the way premiums and subsidies are calculated is unlikely to change anytime soon, though funding for the subsidies themselves is consistently under threat.

To get a sense of how much an ACA plan might cost, visit Health care.gov or your state exchange site and enter your location, your family size and ages, and your expected post-work optional income. (Remember that if you sell a share of stock for $150 that you paid $100 for, only $50 of that is income.) Health care premiums and subsidies are based off a number called your modified adjusted gross income (MAGI), a number that does not appear anywhere on your tax return. Essentially, it's your total income minus deductions for qualified retirement plans like 401(k)s and IRAs, as well as any alimony you paid, and any student loan interest you're eligible to deduct from your taxable income. If you receive Social Security for disability (SSDI or SSI), you have to add this number to your income as well. Note that your MAGI will be larger than your taxable income because it does not factor in the IRS standard deduction or any itemized deductions. After entering your anticipated MAGI, you can compare plan options available in your area to get a sense of coverage levels and costs, and you can click through to determine which providers are on which network. These numbers can change quite a bit year to year, but going through this exercise is helpful for initial budgeting. Having a rough sense of your out-of-pocket costs for health care will be helpful as we build out your customized roadmap in chapter 7.

For years before Mark and I retired we'd been monitoring the costs of health plans on California's state exchange for couples in our age bracket for the income range we expected to have in early retirement, and we adjusted our projected future budget accordingly as rates changed each year. We thought we would be just fine on the most basic silver-level Blue Cross HMO plan offered, but by the time we were actually signing up, Mark was taking a medication that costs $1,000 a month in generic form. If we'd gone with the plan we had expected to get, his medication alone would have cost us $300 a month. But by going instead with the Blue Shield PPO plan with more generous drug coverage—a plan that cost $250 more per month than the HMO option—we got his drug cost down to $15 a month while also bringing our overall out-of-pocket maximum and several copays down. It was an important lesson not just to look at the premium amounts but to dig into the plan details to make sure you select the health insurance that best fits your particular situation and health care needs.

Managed Care Plans

In some parts of the country, particularly larger urban areas, you may have managed care plans available to you that you can buy directly through a health care provider like Kaiser Permanente. These plans function much like traditional health insurance in that you have premiums, copays, and deductibles, but you're usually more restricted to seeing only doctors in network, and you may have to see your primary care physician any time you wish to be referred to a specialist. While these plans tend to be priced comparably to ACA exchange plans, they are worth researching if you have a good managed care network where you live to see which option is more cost-effective in your specific circumstances.

Health Care Sharing Ministries

Health care sharing ministries are not actually insurance but provide members with shared beliefs, usually Christian, with a way to pool resources to pay for members' health care expenses above a deductible of a few thousand dollars. These plans can be significantly cheaper than ACA exchange plans, but with several important caveats: They often require sign-off from a pastor affirming church membership, they disallow smoking and drinking alcohol, and they don't cover expenses from activities deemed immoral, such as drunk driving injuries. Because they aren't actually insurance, they aren't required to cover care for preexisting conditions. There's also no regulation or oversight of these plans, and several states including Montana and Kentucky have attempted to shut the ministries down after they failed to pay members' medical bills. If you're young, healthy, and qualify for membership, health care share ministries may be a good option for you for a few years, but do your homework carefully and research the organization you're thinking of signing on with to be sure there aren't reports of them not paying as promised.

Health Care Tourism

As health care costs continue to skyrocket in the US, doctors and facilities around the world are opening their arms to Americans and other Westerners who wish to save money on planned procedures. While you can't fly to India to have urgent surgery after a car accident, if you know you need a hip replacement, you can shop around in numerous countries who cater to health care tourists. These facilities are modern, and the staff are every bit as well trained as medical staff in the US, making this type of care safe and a fraction of the cost you'd pay in the US, often even after insurance has paid its portion. Early retirees are in a unique position to be able to take part in real health care tourism because we have the time and freedom to travel and to allow time for recuperation before flying home, something that might deplete all of an average worker's sick time and vacation time. A perfect way to try out health care tourism without committing to anything major is to schedule a dental cleaning when you're visiting a country like Mexico, Thailand, Taiwan, or nearly any country in Eastern Europe. The cost will add up to a few dollars, and you can judge for yourself whether you'd like to schedule more of your health and dental care to coincide with overseas travel. Health care tourism is not a good solution for emergency medical care or care for chronic conditions, but it can be an excellent and more cost-effective supplement to your stateside health care for procedures you can plan relatively far in advance.

Jeremy Jacobson and Winnie Tseng retired in their 30s and decided to become full-time nomads, occasionally spending extended periods in her native Taiwan, and in the course of their travels they've used health care and dental services all over the world. They've seen doctors and dentists in Mexico, received urgent care in Malaysia, visited an emergency room in Portugal, undertaken a series of planned procedures in Taiwan, and had follow-up care in Italy. And in all cases, they've felt well taken care of in modern facilities, while paying a fraction of what similar care would have cost in the US.

Tricare/Veterans Administration Health Care

For those who've served in the Armed Services, you have far better health care options at your disposal than most Americans—as you should. (Thank you for your service.) Military and ex-military health care through Tricare and the VA is among the most affordable care available in the US, and while care quality can vary from one VA center to another, patient cost is typically quite low for both medical care and prescription drugs. If you're planning to retire early from the military, consider timing your departure to coincide with when you qualify for lifetime health care benefits along with a pension. The money you save on health care alone could make working one or two additional years extremely worthwhile.

Medicare

Like Social Security, Medicare is an extremely complicated topic, which even many Medicare recipients do not fully understand. There are entire books just on Medicare. The key things to note about it are that it is available to every American at age 65 (don't miss that enrollment date when they send you the letter, or things get complicated), and that it does not cover everything. It's a fallacy to look at ACA exchange plan costs and think, *Oh, I can't wait until I qualify for Medicare. Then I'll be set!* The average Medicare recipient still pays more than $250,000 between turning 65 and the end of their life. For most people, Medicare will cover about 60% of their medical costs, leaving them on the hook for the rest. To put that in perspective, in 2016 more than a quarter of all dollars paid out in Social Security benefits went to paying medical bills above and beyond what Medicare covers. It also doesn't cover the full cost of prescription drugs or doctor's visits, and while Part A covering hospitalizations is free, Parts B and D, which cover doctors and medications, can come with high premiums of several hundred dollars per month. But, despite its shortcomings, Medicare is guaranteed health coverage for everyone 65 and older, and it doesn't discriminate against you for preexisting conditions. It's no small relief to know that you'll always have at least some health coverage for your later years. One way to approach future Medicare costs is not to count Social Security income in your traditional retirement projections, and use the Social Security income you do receive as your health care costs buffer.

For most early retirees and semiretirees in the US, your primary health care choices will come before age 65, with Medicare as the default thereafter unless you have better coverage through military retirement or an especially generous employer retirement package. Keep these options in mind as we move into the next stage of planning.

HOUSING AND HEALTH CARE CHECKLIST

- ☐ Determine whether you want to change your living situation now, to save faster.
- ☐ Decide what your living arrangement will be in early retirement.
- ☐ Formulate a rough plan for housing in traditional retirement or as a backup plan if your needs change.

☐ Ensure you have the right health care coverage now.

☐ Open a health savings account if you have a high-deductible plan and save what you can in it.

☐ Calculate potential future health care costs based on current exchange or Medicare data so that you can account for them in your financial planning.

CHAPTER 6

The Factors That Dictate How Much You Need to Save

You only have to do a very few things right in your life so long
as you don't do too many things wrong.

—Warren Buffett

At this stage, you might be feeling excited about some aspects of
your vision—maybe you're feeling fired up to learn more about real
estate investing, or you're in love with the vision you've created for
your semiretirement—but you're also feeling unsure about how you
go from these big conceptual ideas to a concrete financial plan. Fear
not! In this chapter, we're going to go through all the remaining
decisions that shape your plan. Think of this chapter as building the
shell and mechanical components of the car that will get you going
on your journey, and in the next chapter we'll fill it with gas and get
on the road.

This chapter provides a number of cautions, and the point of
them isn't to scare you but rather to ensure that your financial plan
is rock solid, based on sound reasoning and a realistic assessment
of the risks that are out there. Understanding the biggest risks that
you could face as an early retiree if you don't plan for them will help
you craft a plan that lets you sleep well at night, knowing you've
accounted for every potential pitfall. Think of it as making sure your

car is properly equipped with seat belts and airbags. Knowing you're driving down the road in a safety-minded vehicle is an enormous confidence booster.

Which form of early retirement you're envisioning will tell you where you're pointing this car, so let's review the different versions you could aim for: full early retirement, in which you save enough through magic money–generating vehicles that you never need to earn another penny through work again; semiretirement, in which you save enough so that you have your traditional retirement savings covered and decide how much of your early retirement expenses you want to cover via magic money and how much to cover with ongoing work; and career intermission, in which you save enough to take an extended break from work without jeopardizing your long-term financial well-being.

The Phases of Your Financial Life

Regardless of which form of work-optional living you're planning for, think about your financial life from this point forward as being divided into three primary phases:

1. The **accumulation phase**, when you'll do most of your saving and investing, and when work may still be a big part of your life. The more you earn and the less you spend, the shorter you can make this phase. If you're aiming for a series of career intermissions, you might revisit this phase several times.
2. The **early retirement phase**, when you'll live the dream of the work-optional model you're aiming for, whether that's full early retirement, semiretirement, or career intermission.

3. The **traditional retirement phase**, beginning in your 60s or 70s, when you'll work less or not at all, and the sources of your income and health care will likely shift.

How much you need to save for phases 2 and 3, and in what investment and savings vehicles, is dependent primarily on two factors: which form of early retirement you're aiming for and how much your work-optional life costs. The less it costs, the less you need to save, and the faster you'll get to your destination. There's also the question of how much to save in each investment vehicle, for example, how much to invest in your tax-advantaged retirement accounts versus in regular index funds in your taxable brokerage account, given that there are restrictions around when and how you can access funds in your 401(k) and traditional IRA. Just as you're now thinking of your financial future in phases, you need to decide whether you'd also like to treat your work-optional life as one phase or two:

1. Plan for a **true two-phase retirement**, with two distinct pools of investments and income streams: (1) your taxable investments, rental property, and any passive business ventures generating the magic money to fund your early retirement, and (2) your tax-advantaged retirement accounts and Social Security funding your traditional retirement.
2. Plan for **early and traditional retirement as a single phase**, and save as much as you can in the accumulation phase in the most tax-advantaged ways possible—e.g., maxing out your 401(k) and IRA—and then employ legal tax strategies to access that money before you turn 59½, so that you're essentially saving just one big pool of funds.

Which approach you choose depends on where you're starting. For example, you may already have a large amount saved in tax-advantaged retirement funds but feel more comfortable leaving those funds in place for your later years in traditional retirement rather than tapping them early. Mark and I decided to go with the first option, a two-phase retirement, to give ourselves extra peace of mind in knowing that even if we accidentally overspend in our early retirement years, we'll still be financially secure with our untouched tax-advantaged retirement accounts later on, when we're less able to go out and earn more money if we need it. It would be my worst nightmare to realize when I'm 75 that we undersaved, when there isn't a whole lot we can do about it. Like with our choice to pay off the mortgage, this approach was borne more out of fear than financial savviness, because we know that we're people who enjoy spending money on dining and travel and could at some point stumble and bust the budget. To play to our strengths while accounting for our weaknesses, we crafted a two-phase plan that gives us assurances of still having funds available when we're older. In our case, we also saved a disproportionally large share of our retirement funds for our traditional retirement, so that we can enjoy a few more splurges like nicer hotel rooms and meals out, and so that we'll be well padded against potentially high health care and long-term care costs. But to structure our plan that way, we're living a bit leaner in our early retirement years, and we worked a year or two longer than we would have needed to if we weren't trying to give future us a bigger cushion.

If you know you're more risk averse and crave financial security above everything, aiming for a two-phase retirement will give you the comfort you seek. If working toward a plan with a bit less certainty built into it doesn't scare you and you want to get to your work-optional life as fast as possible, then aim for the single phase. Just make sure your partner is on board, if you're in a couple, because it's not uncommon for partners to differ on this point. When in doubt, there's no downside to being just a little more conservative with your money. Worst case, you oversave and you can leave a big charitable bequest to your favorite cause after you're gone, or you can pass a big chunk down to your descendants. Even though it means having worked a little longer than you might have needed to, I'd choose oversaving but never having to worry about money every day of the week. But the choice is yours.

Accessing Your Traditional Retirement Funds in Early Retirement

To make the decision about whether to aim for a true two-phase retirement or a single-phase retirement, it helps to understand the rules about how you can access your tax-advantaged money early and legally. (Before you actually begin to withdraw funds under either of these approaches, please consult a tax attorney who can review your plan to ensure you're meeting all of the current IRS requirements, which do occasionally change. There's room for creativity in most areas of your early retirement planning, but not when it comes to the Internal Revenue Service.) If these options feel too complicated or confusing, you never need to use them. In that case, aim for a two-phase retirement with separate pools of funds or sources of magic money for each, as Mark and I did. If a single-phase approach feels better to you, then you'll want to understand your early withdrawal options.

All of the tax-advantaged retirement accounts that exist in the US have the same general rules about taking money out, with some important exceptions: You can't touch that money under normal circumstances until the exact day you turn 59½, and if you do that and take what's called an early distribution, you pay a 10% penalty on top of whatever regular income tax you owe on the money. That penalty exists to ensure people don't blow through their retirement savings too early, which is generally a good policy idea, because most people are dramatically unprepared for retirement and it's in our interest as a nation to care for our seniors, who may be struggling to survive. That's why the tax benefit is there in the first place, and why the penalty is there, too: to incentivize saving the money and holding on to it until retirement. There are a few ways you can access the money early through what are considered qualified distributions, many of which aren't very appealing: You become permanently disabled, you use the money to cover especially high medical bills that would be tax-deductible, you turn 55 years old at a job with a 401(k) and can then access only that 401(k) money, or you use the money to pay child support or alimony. In addition, most employer-based plans do not allow you to take any money out while still employed there.

Despite all of those rules, there are two ways for early retirees to access tax-advantaged funds before age 59½ if you're willing to jump through a few hoops, which might be your best option to achieve a work-optional life if you've saved the bulk of your early retirement funds in tax-advantaged traditional retirement accounts. With either of these early withdrawal approaches, you will owe income tax in that tax year on any money you withdraw from an account that you'd funded with pretax dollars, so keep that in mind.

Substantially Equal Periodic Payments

The first option is to take substantially equal periodic payments (SEPP), as specified in IRS Rule 72T. Under this approach, you may take annual payments out of your tax-advantaged funds at any age so long as you continue taking those annual payments at least until you turn 59½ and calculate the payment amounts through one of three IRS-approved computation methods, each of which assumes a life span for you and assumes that you will receive the payments for the remainder of your life. To give you a ballpark sense of how this works, if you begin taking SEPP payments at age 50, the IRS says you most likely have about 34 years left to live, and therefore you'll withdraw approximately 1/34th of your tax-advantaged fund per year, or just under 3%. The actual amount you'll withdraw is based on which computation method you use, for example the required minimum distribution method, which dictates drawing down a percentage of your starting portfolio balance like in the 50-year-old example, or the amortization method, in which you apply the current federal funds interest rate to your starting portfolio balance to determine what amount you'd need to withdraw per year to zero out your account by the end of the IRS-projected life span for you. There's also an annuitization computation method, and it's even more complex. These calculations can be confusing, so it's best to consult a tax attorney before you begin taking SEPPs to ensure you're choosing the computation method that makes the most sense for your situation and applying it correctly.

Taking SEPPs is the fastest way to access your retirement funds, but it has some significant downsides. First, after you begin taking distributions, you cannot discontinue payments or alter the amount to suit your needs each year, for example, if you want to keep your income under a certain threshold for income tax or health care premium purposes. Second, you may not change the computation method you used to calculate your distribution amount for at least five years, and only then if you have reached the age of 59½ already. (The IRS does allow for you to change the computation one time, but only that once, and you cannot stop taking payments as a result of the new calculation.) Third, if you change anything, the 10% early distribution penalty will be applied retroactively to every year of payments you've already received. A big positive is that you don't need to apply the SEPP rules to all of your retirement accounts, so if you have a 401(k) and a separate IRA, you can take SEPPs from one account and leave the rest of your funds alone to avoid having more income than you want. To learn more about the methods for calculating SEPP distribution amounts, see the resources listed in the "Additional Resources" section that will help you make more detailed calculations.

Roth Conversions

The second approach to accessing tax-advantaged funds early is to use the special rules afforded to Roth IRAs. Because Roth accounts are funded by post-tax dollars, they have some advantages that are especially beneficial to early retirees. All of your contributions to Roth accounts have already been taxed, and therefore there is no 10% penalty nor additional income tax if you withdraw those contributions before you turn 59½, which you can legally do anytime. This is only true for the contributions you've made, however, and not the gains that those contributions have earned, which are subject to the same rules as other tax-advantaged accounts and cannot be withdrawn without penalty until you turn 59½. If you plan ahead and save heavily in Roth accounts while you're in your accumulation phase, you may arrive at early retirement with a healthy balance of contributions you can start tapping immediately, while letting the gains continue to compound and grow until you turn 59½, when you can then access them tax-free as well. That doesn't mean, however, that maxing out your Roth accounts while working is automatically in your best interest, assuming you are within the income limits and have the option available to you to contribute directly. (There is a legal loophole known as a backdoor Roth contribution, in which you first invest post-tax dollars in a traditional IRA and then convert that account to Roth later, contributing indirectly. This is an option for those above the income limits.) Because Roths are post-tax dollars, you get no tax break when you make the contribution, only when you later withdraw the contribution and gains tax-free. So unless you're in a very low tax bracket now, there's a good chance that you'll come out ahead maxing out your 401(k) and traditional IRA first, both of which decrease your income taxes when you contribute, and only add to Roth accounts if you've maxed those and still have more to save.

But if you arrive at early retirement and have little to no money already in a Roth, you have another option for accessing your tax-advantaged funds early, which is to take advantage of rules that allow what's known as a Roth conversion. You are permitted to convert funds from a pretax retirement account like a 401(k) or an IRA to a Roth IRA, and then pay the income tax you owe on the amount you converted in that tax year. As long as you don't use any part of the converted amount to pay the income tax you owe for the conversion, there's no 10% penalty so long as you meet one stipulation: The converted funds you withdraw must have been in your Roth account for five years. (And, again, all gains must stay in your account until age 59½ unless you are comfortable paying the penalty.)

It's generally smart to convert small amounts each year so that you don't accidentally bump yourself up into a higher tax bracket, but building a sequence of conversions each year that you can access penalty-free five years later provides an excellent way to tap your retirement funds early. And unlike with the SEPP approach, there's no rule that you have to continue your conversions or distributions. You can convert some amount one year, skip the next year, convert again the following year, or stop converting altogether. And you can withdraw money ("take a distribution") once each conversion reaches the five-year mark, or you can leave it alone to grow, especially if the markets are down and you don't want to lock in losses. The Roth conversion approach has the waiting period as a significant hurdle, but you make up for it with much more flexibility than with the SEPP approach. One note for those who have considered or done Roth conversions in the past: The 2017 tax reform law

removed the old "recharacterization" rule, so now once you've done
a Roth conversion, it's irreversible, and you can't move those dollars
back to a traditional IRA.

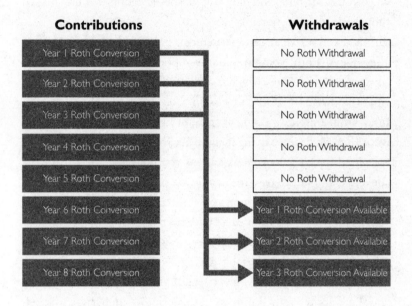

Remember that just because you convert some funds to Roth
doesn't mean you have to spend that money five years later, or at any
point. You can convert a bit each year if you have room within your
tax bracket and within health insurance premium cut-offs, both to
reduce future tax liability and to avoid being forced to take required
minimum distributions (RMDs) when you turn 70½, and then
just let that money grow until your later years. All tax-advantaged
retirement accounts except Roths require you to start taking RMDs
at 70½, and if you'd prefer to keep that money in tax-advantaged
accounts longer, then building up your Roth balance is a smart
move. But remember as well that being forced to take a distribution

from your IRA or 401(k) doesn't mean you're being forced to spend that money, only that you're required to pay income taxes on it at that point. You can take those required distributions and reinvest them instantly in index funds, more real estate, or anything else to continue generating magic money for you, and you'll only ever owe additional tax on those investments' subsequent capital gains.

For all of your other magic money sources that aren't tax-advantaged, tapping them is much simpler. For stocks, bonds, and mutual funds, including index funds held in taxable brokerage accounts, you simply collect dividends and pay income tax on the dividends, and when you sell shares, you pay only long-term capital gains tax—a lower rate than regular income tax—as long as you've owned the shares at least 12 months. If you own rental real estate, you collect rent and only owe income tax on the portion remaining after you subtract out mortgage interest, insurance, maintenance expenses, and property depreciation, which most tax preparation software will calculate for you. None of those magic money sources come with tax penalties, only regular income taxes on the portions that count as income, so converting them from investments to cash flow is much more straightforward than with your tax-advantaged accounts.

Understanding Safe Withdrawal Rates

Deciding how you'll phase your retirement naturally leads to the biggest question of all: *How much do I need to save?* If you're interested primarily in market investing, it turns out the answer requires some reverse engineering, because to determine how much you need to save, you first need to understand how much you can safely withdraw from your total investment portfolio each year without depleting it too quickly. Economists have long been curious how much people need to save to retire securely and to be assured that they won't outlive their money, a legitimate fear that causes many seniors tremendous anxiety. The problem, of course, is that no one can see the future. We don't know what the stock and bond markets will do next week, let alone next year or multiple decades from now. So we can't say with certainty how much is a foolproof amount, nor what percentage of your investments you can spend each year with an iron-clad guarantee that you'll never run out. But the good news is that a great deal of economic analysis has been done that gives us some solid guidelines to plan around, based on looking at past trends in the stock markets and extrapolating out the worst-case scenarios for retirees.

The most well-known study of safe withdrawal rates (SWR) was the Trinity study, published in 1998, which assumed a retirement of 15–30 years and a portfolio composed of at least 50% stocks and stock funds. The study authors concluded that withdrawing 3–4% of a total portfolio at the start of retirement, and then adjusting that figure upward each year by the consumer price index (CPI) inflation percentage, would be safe enough to withstand extended market downturns like we've seen in the past, and the retiree could have confidence that they would not outlive their money. That study is not without its critics, and there are those who argue for both higher and lower safe withdrawal rates, or for approaches to withdrawals that look more closely at what the markets are doing at that moment, but using 3–4% gives us a good starting point to estimate how much you'll need to save.

If we use 3% as the safe withdrawal rate we're targeting, your savings goal for full early retirement would be approximately 33 times the amount you'd like your investments to generate in magic money each year, or 33 times your full annual budget. (For other early retirement models, it could be quite a bit less, as we'll discuss in chapter 7.) If we use 4% as the target SWR, your savings goal is

25 times your annual magic money goal. The difference between those two goals is about eight times your annual expenses, which is not likely to be a small amount. But keep in mind that most studies of safe withdrawal rates have only modeled returns for traditional retirees who stop working in their 60s, assuming at most 30 years of retirement. Early retirement, however, potentially has a much longer time horizon than traditional retirement, and it's worth accounting for that. Early retirees may be looking at 40, 50, or even 60 years of retirement, and because there are so many unknown unknowns in that timeframe, it's worth your while to be cautious. Some experts recommend shifting your safe withdrawal rate to 3% if you retire at 50 or younger, to 3.3% at 55, 3.5% at 60, and 4% or more only for those retiring at 65 or older.[1] And you could certainly make the case that those retiring younger than 35 should be even more conservative, targeting a safe withdrawal rate under 3%, meaning you'd want to save 35 to 40 times your annual expenses—or choose a semiretirement approach that gives you some income coming in each year, even if you're only working on a very part-time basis, to hedge against long-term risk to your portfolio principal. Other analysis shows that a 3.5% safe withdrawal rate provides enough assurance against running out of money and is adequate for most early retirees.[2] At this SWR, you'll save 29–30 times your annual spending for full early retirement, and less for other models.

With stock markets averaging long-term returns between 9 and 11%, depending on which index you track, it's certainly a valid question why it's not safe to withdraw closer to 9–10% of your portfolio each year. And there are four main reasons: (1) Your total portfolio should include not just stock funds, but also bond funds and cash, as they help offset the volatility of stocks, and give you shares you can sell and dollars you can spend when the stock markets are down. But because bonds have lower yields than stocks, and cash returns almost nothing, both reduce your average annual returns in proportion to how large a share of your portfolio they represent. (2) The long-term average returns assume that you're always reinvesting dividends, that is, using the profits the stock shares generate to buy more shares. Because you owe income tax on those dividends, in retirement it makes much more sense to use the dividends as cash flow instead of reinvesting them. This also reduces your annual average returns. (3) Inflation consumes a good portion of those market gains each year, averaging between 2 and 3%, shaving off an additional chunk. Analysis shows that real returns for the stock markets average 6.8% per year.[3] (4) Sequence of returns risk can sink a retirement quickly and unpredictably, and warrant taking a more conservative approach to saving.

Sequence of returns risk, often short-handed as sequence risk, is the risk that bad stock market years early in your retirement will deplete your portfolio so significantly that it will never be able to recover, and you'll run out of money. Because compounding is such a significant factor both in your accumulation phase and in your two retirement phases, you need it working in your favor. When the stock markets crash or stay down for an extended period in retirement, you're not only not getting the benefit of positive compounding, you're actually getting hit by negative compounding, because you're having to sell more shares than you would have in positive growth years, locking in your losses permanently and limiting the growth potential of your now smaller pool of shares. Negative compounding sounds scary, but it's a normal part of retirement and a year of negative growth isn't cause for panic. While we can talk about long-term averages of the stock markets, the reality is that virtually no years actually return gains in line with the average. There are usually many more up years than down years, but a historical market chart looks much more zigzaggy than linear.

The large majority of traditional retirees experience mostly positive gains in their first decade of retirement—the crucial years with regard to sequence risk—and have nothing to worry about. For them, a safe withdrawal rate of 4% will likely end up being unnecessarily

S&P 500 YEAR-END RETURNS

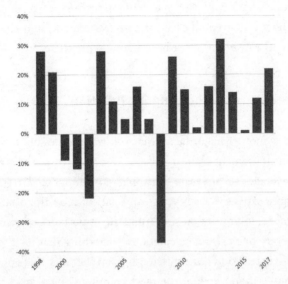

Source: Standard & Poor's

conservative. Research shows that for retirees who don't hit bad returns years early in retirement, a safe withdrawal rate of almost 7% of their starting balance, adjusted upward for inflation each year, is perfectly reasonable. The problem is that we can only know who these retirees are in hindsight. You have to save for retirement not knowing if there will be a major market crash or extended recession early in your retirement—a bad sequence of returns, meaning multiple years of bad returns—and can't bank on being one of the lucky ones who doesn't hit a bad sequence. What's more, economist Karsten Jeske has found that early retirees are far more likely than traditional retirees to experience bad sequences of returns because their targets are usually number-based, not date-based. Traditional retirees leave work at a particular age or when they've hit their pension milestone. But early retirees have high odds of retiring near the end of a bull market—because those positive return years for the stock markets are what propel them to their goal number—and into a recession. That's why it pays to be more conservative when determining how much you'll save for early retirement, and the earlier you retire, the more conservative it makes sense to be.

Accounting for Inflation

Inflation is another major factor that you want to be sure to account for in your retirement planning. I've said several times already that it tends to average 2–3% a year—meaning most things tend to get about 2–3% more expensive each year—and part of repeating that stat so many times is to imprint on your mind the importance of accounting for it in every one of your calculations, something that requires us to see the financial world quite differently from the story that's out there. For example, if you look at the most commonly cited stock market index, the Dow Jones Industrial Average, the chart of absolute (nominal) growth over the last century looks incredibly dramatic:

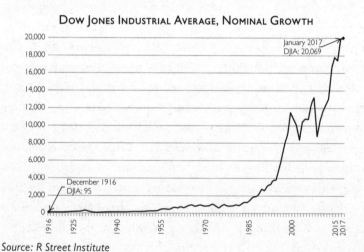

DOW JONES INDUSTRIAL AVERAGE, NOMINAL GROWTH

Source: R Street Institute

However, that chart looks only at the absolute price, sometimes called the "nominal return," a metric that's essentially worthless to the average investor. Why? Because it doesn't cost the same amount to buy something now as it cost in 1916 when the Dow was at 95 points and the largest company stocks cost pennies. What you care about is the real return, or the inflation-adjusted number that puts things into terms that relate to today's dollars or future dollars. In the last century, during which the Dow has had what looks like explosive growth, we've also had inflation of approximately 3.25% per year, a rate that results in prices doubling every 20 years, for a grand total of more than 2,000% inflation over the last century. (Something that cost $1 in the 1910s now costs more than $20.) When you adjust the Dow for that inflation, the chart looks quite different:

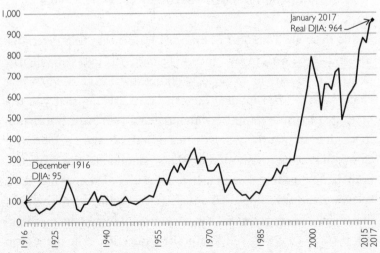

DOW JONES INDUSTRIAL AVERAGE, REAL GROWTH

(CONSTANT 1916 DOLLARS)

Source: R Street Institute

The inflation-adjusted average, in 1916 dollars, puts the Dow at only about 1,000 points today, not above 20,000. And that's still significant growth over time—well more than the rate of inflation—but in real terms, not nominal terms, the difference is far smaller than what the typical stock market charts reflect. This second chart also shows why the stock market is not the right place to park money you expect to need in the next few years, say for a home down payment or car purchase, because it may take many years to see gains on your investments in real terms.

Fortunately, there are some easy ways to adjust for inflation in your planning that don't require a ton of mind-bending, and I'll remind you when to account for it as we build out your plan, often by using real returns instead of nominal returns. Inflation is an ever-present force eroding the purchasing power of every dollar, but as long as you always account for it, you'll be in good shape.

Accounting for Both Partners' Comfort Levels

While there are a number of financial factors that help determine how much you need to save, there are emotional factors as well, particularly if you are in a couple. Working toward the freedom that comes with a work-optional life can be so exciting that you feel motivated to move toward it without giving your partner a chance to weigh in substantively, and that's a mistake. Make a point to stay closely in sync on every aspect of your work-optional financial plan, both the big goal of how much you'll save and the smaller daily spending and investing decisions. If you're hitting your goals but one of you feels resentful for having to give up something meaningful, that's not moving you in a positive direction. The more open you can both be in communicating your feelings about how much you want to be able to spend in your work-optional life, how much work your plan should include, what safe withdrawal rate feels comfortable to you, and how much investment risk you're comfortable taking on, the better.

It helps to accept at the outset that it's going to be a learning process, one in which you'll both grow a ton together. But if you focus on staying on the same page financially and emotionally from the very beginning of your early retirement planning and at every step along the way, it'll be one in which you grow much closer, because achieving something as momentous as early retirement has a truly transformative effect. In these discussions, make sure you talk about each of your visions for when you'll retire, cut back at work, or take your career intermission. Unless one partner truly loves their work and can't imagine giving it up, or one partner plays a full-time caregiver role to children, it makes the most sense for both partners to retire early, semiretire, or go on career intermission as close to the same time as possible. First, the retired partner can't travel or get the benefit of company during their newfound free time, and that can lead to boredom and aimlessness, which is not the ideal way to begin early retirement. And second, the partner stuck still working is likely to feel resentful of the other partner's freedom. Research shows that spouses who retire at different times have more challenges adjusting to work-optional life than do those who make the leap together. In particular, the spouse who retires first is much more vulnerable to social isolation.[4] But you both know your own situation best and can decide what timing makes the most sense for you and how that will affect the amount you'll save.

In our case, it was clear early on that we wanted to retire at the same time, though we did have to discuss it several times before we agreed. Mark is three years older than I am and understandably felt that it was unfair that I would end up working for fewer years than he would. But when we considered the alternative—he having fun and sometimes being bored without me, and I feeling resentment at having to work while he was out playing—it was obvious that retiring together was the best option by far. In addition, I'm much more financially conservative than Mark is, thinking about every possible worst-case scenario that could happen (that's a good thing for you because it means this book is comprehensive on managing risk), while he's comfortable living with much more investment volatility. If he had created our "magic number" purely based on his preferences, it would have been quite a bit lower than I was comfortable with, because he doesn't need quite as many built-in contingencies as I do to sleep well at night. But knowing that his version of the plan would stress me out and make it hard to enjoy our early retirement, we bumped our number up and arrived at a target that felt comfortable to both of us.

If you're planning for early retirement as a couple, make sure you're making these decisions on plan mechanics together, just as you are all the other big planning decisions.

EARLY RETIREMENT FACTORS CHECKLIST

- ☐ Decide whether you'll pursue a two-phase early retirement or save for a singular phase.
- ☐ If you are planning for a singular phase, determine conceptually whether you'll need to use SEPPs or Roth conversions to access tax-advantaged money early, based on how much you already have saved and what investment vehicles you'll use moving forward.
- ☐ Decide whether you would like to plan for a more conservative safe withdrawal rate (3–3.5%) or a more aggressive one (4%).
- ☐ Make all of these decisions jointly with your partner, if you have one.

CHAPTER 7

Your Financial Roadmap to a Work-Optional Life

The secret to getting ahead is getting started.
—Mark Twain

It's time to look at your actual money, which is perhaps the most fun part of all, because this is when things get real. You are really creating a plan and moving toward a work-optional life. Best of all, we're going to break everything down into achievable milestones and give you systems to put in place to ensure you succeed. When Mark and I first mapped out how much we'd need to save to leave our careers behind, a small voice in my head wondered, *Can we really do that?!* Especially for someone like me who'd never been good at saving money, I couldn't actually imagine mustering up the willpower to put every one of those dollars away. Fortunately, with a clear plan in place and systems taking all the guesswork out of it, I didn't need that willpower, and neither do you. So don't worry if you feel some doubt, because that's normal. And this chapter will prove to you that you can achieve your goal.

As we proceed through building your financial plan, keep in mind that this is meant to be a living document that evolves as you make progress. You may find, for example, as you scrutinize your spending and expenses over time, that you need less to be happy than you thought you did, and your goal amount may shrink. You may realize that you've cut too much out of your spending and feel deprived, and decide to raise your goal number a bit. Likewise your timeline may shorten or lengthen as you see the tailwind effect from your market investments or as you decide to add more contingencies to your plan. All of that is normal, too—and good. The roadmap we create here will be something you continually refine up until the day you embark on your work-optional life. Creating your roadmap isn't about locking you into a track you can't step out of, it's about giving your money purpose and direction and getting you to your best life ASAP.

Central to all of this is the question of what is *enough*. When you have enough, you no longer need to keep working, and you can step aside to create opportunity for someone else. When you have enough, you can cover all of your needs and enough of your wants that you feel excited to live your life. When you have enough, you don't lose sleep or stress about money anymore. When you have enough, offers of more money don't mean much, because you're already set for life. The trick is not to confuse *enough* and *too much*. You've already done some thinking about your life and your spending and have no doubt identified some things you have spent money on that didn't ultimately make you any happier. Those fall into the category of too much, and the more of those things you can let go of, the faster you'll be able to save, and the less you'll need to rest in the knowledge that you'll always have enough.

Your Current Financial Picture

So let's get granular, starting with your current financial picture. Do you know how much you're currently spending? Do you follow a budget? Research shows that 60% of Americans don't keep a budget, so you're in good company if you aren't a budgeter, but to get on the road to a work-optional life, you want to get total clarity about where your finances stand now. A great place to begin is calculating your net worth. That's your starting line against which you'll track all progress moving forward. Your net worth is your assets minus your liabilities (debts) and includes:

ASSETS	
Cash savings	
Retirement savings	
Taxable investments	
Home equity	
Other property equity	
Cash value of life insurance	
ASSETS TOTAL	
DEBTS (LIABILITIES)	
Credit card debt	
Mortgage balance	
Car loan balance	
Student loan balance	
Other debt	
DEBTS TOTAL	
TOTAL ASSETS MINUS DEBTS	

Note: I don't recommend including car value as an asset unless you plan to sell that car now, nor the value of all of the possessions that fill your home, because those are depreciating assets that only continue to lose value.

If you don't already have a financial tracking system set up, this is a great time to create a spreadsheet like the one above. In it, tally up all of your assets, and subtract from that number all of your debts. That will give you your current net worth. Create a tab in the spreadsheet where you will update your net worth each month, and use this starting point number as your first entry. And if your starting point number is a negative one, don't get discouraged. Paying off debt is a part of nearly everyone's journey to early retirement.

Tracking Your Spending

The next step is crucial: getting a clear handle on your current spending. It's only after you truly understand where all of your money is going that you can figure out ways to trim more and determine how much you can save toward your goal. Even if you already know roughly how much you're spending in total, which may give you a ballpark sense of your early retirement savings goal, it won't tell you much about your specific habits. To figure that out, you need to look not just at the total but at all of the different places your money goes.

If every dollar you spend comes out of your checking account via check or debit card transaction, then your tracking will be easy, because you already essentially have a ledger of it. But for most of us who spend money with a combination of cash, credit cards, and debit cards, you'll need to combine the transactions from all of those places into one ledger. If you're in a couple, you'll want to include both partners' spending to get the full picture. Fortunately, there is a whole financial technology sector that now exists to help you get your head around every aspect of your money, making it easier than ever to analyze data automatically. The most well-known of the free tracking apps is Mint, but other free and paid options include You Need a Budget (YNAB), Personal Capital, Clarity Money, and Tiller, and new tools come out all the time. Your bank may also offer dashboard tools that will allow you to analyze your spending this way. All of these apps aggregate your data from across your various accounts and then give you a breakdown of where your money is going within broad categories like restaurants, utilities, and entertainment. Seeing that breakdown may be enough to give you an *aha!* moment, as it surely did for us when we first started tracking our spending. We knew we were eating a lot of restaurant food but had no idea how much it all added up to. The shock of seeing how much of our income was going to eating out made it easy for us to decide to cut back. If you get a similar shock, use it. Funnel that energy into making some changes that will point you toward your goals.

To get a true sense of your spending habits, you need to track several months, not just one, because spending fluctuates. Some tracking apps will let you go back a full year, which is extra helpful, though they won't give you any information about things you bought with cash. Looking backward at recent past spending is helpful to confirm those sources of mindless spending and lifestyle inflation you've already identified in part I or to find any hidden sources of mindless spending that you hadn't already found. It's worth digging into the categories to look for any hidden trends and make note of any spending triggers you find in the process.

Then, you want to start tracking your spending moving forward. It's perfectly acceptable to start saving before you have your plan fully baked. Using your new spending philosophy and money mission statement from chapter 3, track your spending for three consecutive months. It may help you to put all your spending on one debit card during the tracking period and avoid using cash, so you have a complete record. If you trust yourself with credit cards and always pay off your balance in full each month, you can put everything on one credit card to simplify your analysis. Don't leave anything out of the tracking, even if it seems like a one-time expense. Sometimes we tell ourselves that we're spending money on something just one time, but when we look across all of our spending, we notice a trend of many one-time expenses. So keep track of every dollar.

While you're tracking the numbers side of it, consider keeping a journal during the same period. It doesn't have to be anything formal. It could just be a note in your phone where you jot things you notice. You may find yourself questioning your spending decisions now that you know that each transaction will be logged, and it's worth noting what feelings come up so you can identify trends. Like if you keep finding yourself wanting to buy clothes online but also turning down invitations to hang out with friends because you're concerned about the cost, make note of those things.

At the end of the tracking period, take some time to go through your numbers and compare them to the notes you recorded. Then ask yourself: Did you stick to your new spending philosophy and money mission statement? How did it feel to do that? Was it too hard to stick to? Was there any mindless spending that still snuck in? Did you feel deprived during the tracking period? Did you feel like there was even more you could trim without having to pinch pennies or making yourself unhappy? If you're in a couple, do this deep dive into your numbers and feelings together. Based on your answers, you might decide to tweak your spending philosophy—and it's perfectly fine if you decide that you want to be less restrictive—or you might luck out and find that your spending during the tracking period felt just right.

The goal of this process is to find your comfortable spending level: an amount you can spend in the present that feels like enough to enjoy your life now while still devoting significant money to reaching your future financial goals. If you put all of your focus on future goals at the expense of enjoying your current life, you'll end up unhappy, and you'll be far more likely to give up on your plan.

It is so much better to reach your goal a little more slowly than you may prefer than to give up on it altogether.

After your tracking tools are set up and you've gotten into the groove of regularly monitoring your spending, you can use those tools continuously to stay accountable to yourself. Schedule a monthly money date with your partner or with yourself, go through your spending to look for any new sources of mindless spending or lifestyle inflation, and check in on how you're feeling and whether you need to tighten things up or give yourself more latitude.

Now that you know your comfortable spending level, extrapolate it out for a full year by multiplying your average monthly spending by 12, and then factor in known expenses that didn't fall during your tracking period, like property taxes or a vacation. With this annual spending total, you can easily determine how much money you have available to devote to your financial goals. Roughly speaking, if you subtract your current comfortable spending level from your annual take-home pay, that's how much you have to devote to paying off debt and saving for early retirement. The actual total available may differ, because some of that money could go toward tax-advantaged accounts like your 401(k), traditional IRA, or HSA. The more you contribute to those accounts, the more you can actually save, because those dollars aren't subject to income tax when you contribute.

That comfortable spending level also gives you a ballpark estimate of how much you need to save, depending on which version of retirement you're aiming for: somewhere between a few years of comfortable spending for a career intermission and 25–35 times your expected future spending (the variable x) for full early retirement. Or, for real estate investing, that comfortable spending level tells you how much income you need your rental properties to generate—either the full amount each year or some fraction of it for a semiretirement goal.

To project forward even more accurately to your spending in your work-optional life, reflect on how the spending in that life might differ from your current spending. It's natural when people retire for some expenses to go down, for example, no longer having commute expenses and not having to buy so many work clothes or pay for dry cleaning. But some expenses naturally go up, like utility charges because you're home more and may need more heat and air-conditioning, more spending on travel because you have time to do it, and more hobby-related spending. Consider the natural expenses that will shift, and add to that the new line items that are particular to your life vision. Factor in the potentially higher health care costs we examined in chapter 5, as well as changes to your living situation, like if you plan to move somewhere cheaper or more expensive. Next consider whether you have any known future one-time expenses, like paying for children's college, supporting an aging loved one, or moving yourself to your dream location. Then think about how often you may need a new (used) car, new appliances in your home, or other large purchases and divide those costs over the number of years you expect between each purchase, and then add to that expected home and car maintenance costs if they aren't already reflected in your spending. It's also smart to add a few thousand dollars a year of padding here for health care given that health care costs are currently rising at three times the rate of inflation. Tally all of that up to determine your x, which will guide your planning.

Comfortable spending level →
Determines how quickly you can save

Future spending (x) →
Determines how much you need to save

walked away from his job after hitting their early retirement magic number, and they switched roles: Mindy now works full-time in a job that she considers pure fun, helping to manage a real estate education website. They don't need her income to live on, because they saved for full early retirement first, and instead they bank everything she earns for the girls' future college education. You might find this to be a helpful model to consider if you're expecting large future expenses.

The Magic Number Calculations for Each Type of Early Retirement

If you think of saving for retirement as a spectrum, on the low end of the savings spectrum is saving for traditional retirement at 65 or 67, and on the high end of the spectrum is full early retirement, in which you save the most. In between those two ends of the spectrum are the other variations of early retirement: career intermission as the next most aggressive goal beyond traditional retirement, with semiretirement as a step up beyond that.

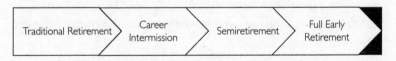

| Traditional Retirement | Career Intermission | Semiretirement | Full Early Retirement |

And remember that these designations aren't absolute. You might plan for one but do another for a while. In our case, we planned for full early retirement but ended up working a little bit in our first year of retirement (including writing this book). Even though we felt early retired, we didn't rely on magic money to pay our bills, so our finances that year more closely resembled semiretirement. But we're still planning to act fully retired one of these days and like knowing that any work we do now is entirely optional and our financial plan doesn't rely on earning another penny.

Taking all of the numbers you've now tallied up—your current comfortable spending level and future spending, your anticipated one-time expenses, and the safe withdrawal rate you're comfortable with—let's dig into the math on how much you would need to save for each form of early retirement.

Full Early Retirement Magic Number

For full early retirement, in which you never need to work again, your goal if you're focusing on any form of market investing is to save between 25 and 35 times your annual expenses by the time you leave active employment, with your actual multiplier dictated by your risk tolerance (more financially conservative equals a safe withdrawal rate of 3.5% or lower). If you're focusing on rental real estate, then your goal is to generate enough magic money after expenses and taxes to cover all of your annual spending. And if you have the benefit of a pension, subtract the amount you expect to receive each year from x in these calculations.

For a quick calculation, you can ballpark a conservative full early retirement magic number as:

$$\text{Annual spending } (x) \times 30 + 10\% \text{ contingency}$$
$$= \text{Full early retirement magic number}$$

That formula builds in some additional buffer against sequence risk by using a lower safe withdrawal rate than 4% and provides additional padding in the form of the contingency that protects against future unknowns like higher health care and housing costs.

For a more detailed calculation, plug in your expected annual spending, the safe withdrawal rate (between 3 and 4%—see chapter 6), and any additional one-time expenses you know you'll need to fund, like children's college education or a home purchase, and then calculate your magic number.

	Annual spending ($)	SWR (%)	Inverse of SWR (100/ SWR)	Base amount (annual expenses × multiplier) ($)	One-time additional expenses ($)	Ballpark magic number ($)
Magic number = annual spending (minus any pension payments) × inverse of safe withdrawal rate + additional expected expenses	x	SWR	100/SWR	100x/SWR	y	100x/ SWR + y

SAMPLE FULL EARLY RETIREMENT SCENARIOS

	Annual spending ($)	SWR (%)	Inverse of SWR (100/ SWR)	Base amount (annual expenses × multiplier) ($)	One-time additional expenses ($)	Ballpark magic number ($)
Scenario 1: Low full early retirement annual expenses of $40,000 per year, high risk tolerance, and no other anticipated large future expenses	40,000	4	25	1,000,000	—	1,000,000

(Continued)

	Annual spending ($)	SWR (%)	Inverse of SWR (100/ SWR)	Base amount (annual expenses × multiplier) ($)	One-time additional expenses ($)	Ballpark magic number ($)
Scenario 2: $50,000 annual expenses, medium risk tolerance, and $60,000 in anticipated kids' college costs	50,000	3.5	31.25	1,562,500	60,000	1,622,500
Scenario 3: $75,000 annual expenses, low risk tolerance, and $200,000 in anticipated kids' college costs and support to aging parents	75,000	3	33.33	2,500,000	200,000	2,700,000

For a rental real estate–focused full early retirement, what you're looking to determine is how much you'll need to invest in properties to generate the magic money that will support your lifestyle. While there's no certainty about how much rent you'll collect on a given property, you can figure out a ballpark figure using this formula:

Annual income needed ÷ cash-on-cash return*
= Principal to invest in real estate for full early retirement

*Cash-on-cash return is the ratio of pretax cash flow on your rental property to the amount of your total investment, expressed as a percentage. It is one of many calculations involved in rental real estate. To get a general sense, ballpark 10% for that figure here or multiply your annual income needed before tax by 10. Consult the "Additional Resources" section of this book for further reading on real estate investing and guidance on how to do it safely and profitably.

In addition to determining your full early retirement magic number, if you're opting for a two-phase retirement like we did, you may also decide to break out your total into what you need for phase 1 (your early retirement) and what you need for phase 2 (traditional retirement), especially if you plan to keep your pools of funds for each phase separate and need different targets. Use the calculations in the semiretirement section below to help you think about the breakout. In our case, we saved extremely conservatively, and retired with a greater share of our investments in our phase 2 investment vehicles (to use after age 59½) even though those funds have time to grow significantly, so that we're able to increase our spending and have ample padding for contingencies in our later years.

HOW MUCH TANJA AND MARK SAVED

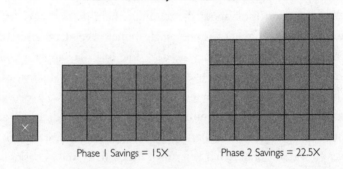

Phase 1 Savings = 15X   Phase 2 Savings = 22.5X

Consider your phased or nonphased approach when deciding not just your overall total, but how it breaks out over different periods of time.

Semiretirement Magic Number

For semiretirement, in which you plan to work part-time or seasonally in early retirement, your goal is slightly more complex to calculate, but will result in a smaller amount. No matter how you approach it, you'll want to save fully for traditional retirement before you transition to semiretirement. However, because you will have some amount of time between when you semiretire and when you reach traditional retirement age, you don't need to save the full 25x to 30x, because the markets will generate much of that growth for you. (We're calling it magic money for a reason, after all.) So your target for traditional retirement is an amount that will compound to 25 or 30 times your annual spending (after accounting for any pensions) by the time you reach age 65 or whatever your full retirement goal age is.

You can then think about the semiretirement portion two different ways: semiretirement with no magic money needed, or semiretirement with some magic money needed. The first may apply if you're currently a high earner and live well below your means. In that case, scaling back on work enough to cover only your comfortable spending level or a similar future spending level may feel like a dramatic and positive reduction. And in that case, you only need to save enough to cover your traditional retirement down the road, as well as basics like an emergency fund and a life happens fund. For that version of semiretirement, this calculation gives you a ballpark of what you need:

25–30x before compounding
= Semiretirement magic number, option 1

Use the Investor.gov calculator listed in the "Additional Resources" section of this book to work backward from your future retire-

ment target and your semiretirement date, using conservative esti-
mates like 2 or 3% real returns. (Because we're calculating this in
today's dollars, you need to adjust for inflation by taking 3% off
the top of your expected gains. And because your portfolio isn't
all stock, you need to further adjust down from historic market averages on stocks only.) Adjust your starting amount until
you reach an end amount that matches what you'll need down
the road, to account for the magic money compounding that will
happen quietly in the background while you enjoy your semiretirement.

For example, assuming 3% real returns annually after inflation,
if you plan to retire fully in 20 years with $1,000,000 in today's
dollars (it will grow to more in future dollars), the calculator says
you need to start with approximately $554,000 saved for traditional
retirement before compounding.

If you are aiming for the second option and hope to have some
magic money cash flow in semiretirement, start by determining how
much you need to save for traditional retirement with the approach
above, and then add to it a calculation of how much additional you
need to save for your near-term spending.

Using a withdrawal calculator like Bankrate's (listed in the "Additional Resources" section of this book), plug in the number of years
you expect to withdraw funds, your expected rate of return (again,
go conservative at 2–3% real returns to be safe), and the amount
you will need each year in today's dollars, and then calculate how
much you'll need to have saved for semiretirement, working backward as you did with the traditional retirement calculation until you
still have a little bit left in your account at the end of your semiretirement period.

For example, if you expect to be semiretired for 20 years and need
$10,000 in today's dollars each year to supplement the income you'll

earn from working, at a 3% real rate of return, you'll need a starting balance for your phase 1 of approximately $155,000.

Combining the two examples, if you expect to save until you can semiretire and then be semiretired for 20 years before retiring fully, your annual expenses are $40,000, and you expect to take home $30,000 after tax in semiretirement, then you'll need to save just over $700,000 before leaving your full-time work, assuming modest market growth over that period. Of course, you may decide to be more bullish and anticipate larger market gains and decide to save less, or be even more financially conservative and opt to save more. Those choices are entirely yours to make.

Just as in the calculations for full semiretirement, add to your magic number the savings you anticipate needing for known one-time expenses like kids' college or a home purchase, and if you have many years between now and then, the Investor.gov calculator can help you figure out how much you need to save so that it will grow to your target amount by the time you need it.

Your combined semiretirement formula is therefore:

Traditional retirement target before compounding +
Semiretirement target before compounding +
One-time expense target before compounding
= Semiretirement magic number, option 2

If you're aiming for full early retirement in two phases, consider adapting this calculation to project for how much to save in your phase 2 tax-advantaged funds (traditional retirement), how much to save in your taxable investments (semiretirement here, but your phase 1 early retirement), and how much padding to add for known expenses.

Career Intermission Magic Number

For career intermission, the amount you'll need to save is much lower than with full early retirement or semiretirement because you're not having to save for the rest of your life before you embark on your adventure. Your goal is simply to save enough that you're on track for permanent financial security and your career intermission doesn't set you back.

Your magic number in this case is based on saving enough to be on track with your traditional retirement savings for your age, plus enough to cover the period of your intermission with an added buffer of at least six months just in case it takes longer than you anticipate to go back to work. Experts disagree on how much you should have saved for retirement by any given age, but the following chart is a good general guide.

RECOMMENDED RETIREMENT SAVINGS, BY AGE

Age 30	Save 1× your salary
Age 35	Save 2× your salary
Age 40	Save 3× your salary
Age 45	Save 4× your salary
Age 50	Save 6× your salary
Age 55	Save 7× your salary
Age 60	Save 8× your salary
Age 67	Save 10× your salary

Source: Fidelity Investments

For example, if you plan to take a career intermission at 40, you should have three times your annual salary saved for retirement before you do, in addition to the non-tax-advantaged funds that will cover your expenses during the intermission itself and the buffer period. But if you expect to take a longer intermission of, say, five years, you want to look at the retirement target for the age when you expect to return, which would be 45. In that case, you'll want to have four times your salary saved for retirement, along with your separate account for intermission expenses and your buffer, before you leave your job. These age-based recommendations assume that your salary goes up over time and that your retirement expenses will be much lower than your expenses while working (so 10× your salary at 67 may equal 20–30 times your retirement spending). If those assumptions don't apply to you, adjust your amounts accordingly.

The calculation for your career intermission magic number is therefore:

Retirement savings age target +
Intermission living expenses +
6–12 months additional expenses =
Career intermission magic number

The companion website to this book, TheWorkOptionalBook .com, has a range of spreadsheets available for you to download to calculate your magic number in more detail and to experiment with a range of market returns. I encourage you to use them as you are building your plan in detail.

Whichever model of work-optional life you're aiming for, you now have a much clearer sense of the magic number you're aiming for, and while you will almost certainly continue to tweak and refine that number over time, having an initial goal gives you a target to aim for, which means you are officially on your way.

Determining Your Sequence of Saving

With your magic number now in hand, let's map out how you actually achieve it and how long that will take. Subtract your current comfortable spending level from your take-home pay to determine how much you can devote per year to saving at this moment. This amount is your goal money, the money that will get you to your goals.

The sequences below provide a starting point for thinking about how to use that goal money to progress toward your work-optional magic number, checking off intermediate goals like debt payoff along the way. Choose your starting point based on where you are currently in your financial journey, and then as you check off each box in the sequence (skip any that don't apply to your situation), you can use your goal money to work toward the next step in the progression until you've eventually completed all of them.

Save $2,000 in an emergency fund.

Contribute enough to your 401(k) to get the full employer match.

Build up your emergency fund to equal 6 months of expenses
(3 months if dual-income household).

Dedicate all additional money to paying off high-interest debt
(anything above 7–8%) until paid off.

Use half of extra funds to increase 401(k) and IRA contributions, and half for accelerated
student and car debt payoff, OR devote half to retirement accounts and half to
down payment savings.

Max out 401(k) and traditional IRA up to annual limits.

Max out your Roth IRA contribution (if eligible by income), or fund a backdoor Roth.

Fully fund your HSA up to annual limits, if you are eligible for one, and kids' 529 accounts.

Invest in taxable investment accounts, primarily index funds.

Pay down your mortgage balance ahead of schedule if you own a home.

Consider contributing to a donor-advised fund.

As the last step before retiring, save enough in cash to fund 2–3 years of full early
retirement or semiretirement, or enough for your career intermission plus buffer.

If you're aiming for a real estate–focused early retirement, your savings sequence may look slightly different:

Save $2,000 in an emergency fund.

Contribute enough to your 401(k) to get the full employer match.

Build up your emergency fund to equal 6 months of expenses (3 months if dual-income household).

Dedicate all additional money to paying off high-interest debt (anything above 7–8%) until paid off.

Save additional funds for rental property purchase and a cash buffer. For each, aim for 20–30 percent down payment plus enough cash to cover 6 months of mortgage payments.

Pay off all non-mortgage debt.

Save for additional rental properties with cash buffers.

Consider maxing your 401(k) or IRA, contributing to a Roth IRA, HSA, or 529, and investing in taxable investment accounts, primarily index funds.

Consider contributing to a donor-advised fund.

Determining Your Timeline

After you have determined how much you need to save and how you'll go about doing it via the saving sequence above, the next question on your mind is *How long will it take?* And if you're feeling especially antsy at work, your question might be *How long until I can quit my job?* It all depends on how quickly you can save, which is answered by these three questions:

1. How much do you currently have left over after you've covered your comfortable spending level?

2. Do you expect your income to increase over time, and if so, by how much?

3. Do you wish to be conservative or aggressive in projecting how quickly your portfolio will grow?

On average, salaried employees can expect about a 3% wage increase each year, with exceptions in recessions. When you factor in the yearly inflation rates of 2–3%, that's essentially treading water. However, that figure doesn't factor in promotions or bonuses, nor does it reflect certain high-skill industries that give significantly larger raises to retain valued talent. So even if 3% raises are typical for you, do you expect to be promoted in the near future, and do you know how much more that might earn you? When you get raises, can you constrain your spending and devote the additional funds to your early retirement goal?

In a scenario in which a person or couple is able to begin by saving $10,000 of goal money per year out of take-home pay of $60,000 (after taxes), the simple power of even modest (5%) market growth will multiply their savings over time, and when we add raises to that, the amounts saved skyrocket.

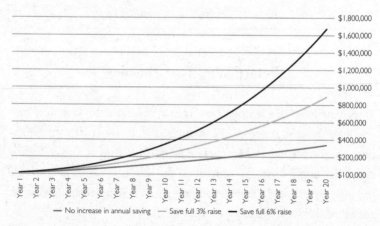

To determine your timeline to early retirement, take the amount you're currently able to save as goal money and factor in your projected pay increases (a spreadsheet is available at TheWorkOptionalBook .com to help you calculate this) to estimate how much you devote to your goals each year moving forward. The magic of investing those raises instead of spending them is that your savings will actually grow far faster than your salary grows, because you're investing and compounding 100% of your marginal salary gains. The chart above shows just how powerful that can be. Very roughly speaking, you can then tally up the cumulative savings year over year until you hit your goal number, but you'll certainly get the benefit of capital gains and compounding to speed you along.

The final step in creating your work-optional financial plan is to expand your spreadsheet to include all the specifics of your situation:

- Your current total income, to factor pretax contributions like 401(k) and IRAs
- Your take-home pay, to factor what's left over in goal money to allocate to all of your line items in the saving sequence
- Your total debt, divided into mortgage, moderate interest debt, and high-interest debt
- Your projected pay increases each year
- Other sources of income that may trigger in the future, such as if you add a rental property that nets a positive cash flow, future pensions, and Social Security (if you're counting it)
- How much you expect to withdraw each year in early retirement (x minus other income sources)

After you add in all of those factors, add them to your spreadsheet (which you can download as a template at TheWorkOptionalBook .com), and determine your saving targets for each year (including debt payoff and intermediate savings goals) so that you'll have a set of intermediate milestones to aim for and celebrate.

While it may take time to fill in the spreadsheet and to create the formulas if you are building it yourself, the great thing about putting in that work is you can then tweak any numbers you want without having to reconfigure the whole sheet. If you want to know, for example, what impact it would have if you switched jobs and began earning $10,000 more a year, you can plug that in and see the effect it has. Just like every element of your plan, this spreadsheet is a living document, and you'll want to revisit it and tweak it numerous times throughout your journey. If the timeline is longer than you'd like it to be, look for places where you can make adjustments, like by reducing your spending more or aiming for semiretirement with some work instead of full early retirement. In chapter 8 we'll talk about ways to earn more, which is another big way to shave off time.

Once you have your spreadsheet filled in, it's also not a bad idea to get a second opinion from a financial pro. There's no rocket science involved in these calculations, but given that the worst-case scenario is running out of money in old age, there's no downside to having someone check your assumptions. Make sure to seek out a certified financial planner (CFP) or advisor who abides by the fiduciary standard, so that they're not getting paid to push products on you. This service may be offered by your bank or brokerage for free, or you may choose to hire an independent, fee-only planner. One tip, though: Many old-school planners don't believe that early retirement is possible, so ask them before you schedule your appointment what their perspective on early retirement is. If they seem open-minded, listen to any concerns they raise and tweak your plan accordingly. If they seem dubious from the outset, though, find another planner to consult. At a minimum, enter your numbers into an online Monte Carlo simulator like cFIREsim that will analyze your odds of having enough saved based on your inputs. If either a planner or simulator suggest you won't have enough, revisit your plan.

Congratulations! You've created version 1 of your plan and your work-optional life is now in sight.

Systems to Ensure You Succeed

We've now gone through a lot of math, which is a critical step in the process of figuring out how much you need for your work-optional life and how long it will take you to get to your destination. But the math itself doesn't tell us much about how we actually make this happen. Money is not just a mathematical thing. Money comes loaded with a whole slew of emotions that differ for each of us, and making the choice to save large amounts of it may trigger feelings of scarcity (*I won't have enough left over to enjoy life*), hopelessness (*I could never save that much*), or self-doubt (*I don't have the willpower to stick to a plan like this*). And that's where systems come in to help you succeed.

I have never been a natural saver, and though I've known lots of people who are perfectly happy living frugally, I can always imagine what I'd spend more money on if I had it. (Top of the list: more travel!) So just as I was the last person you'd expect to retire early, I was the last person *I* ever expected to be able to save a lot of money. I'm not exceptionally disciplined, I don't have superhuman levels of willpower, and I'm absolutely susceptible to temptation and FOMO (fear of missing out). For most of my 20s, I'd spend whatever was in my checking account and just barely make it to the next paycheck before running out of money. It was out of desperation that I discovered the entire key to my financial success, and it had nothing to do with developing more willpower overnight. I knew I needed to save money, but all my attempts at budgeting had failed. I'd set a goal of saving $100 at the end of each month, but when that time came, I had nothing left in my account. Around that time, though, my employer changed payroll systems, and I had to submit new bank account forms. I noticed on the form that I could opt to have my paycheck split into two accounts, and I realized that was my answer: Divert part of each paycheck into savings so that I never even saw that money, the same way I never saw the money that came out for the tiny 401(k) contributions I was making at that time. That was when my strategy of hiding money from myself was born, and when Mark and I got married, we built on that strategy together and let it carry us all the way to early retirement.

Our "hide money from yourself" strategy often goes by the name "pay yourself first"—in other words, saving and investing for your own future before you pay other expenses or splurge on wants. But paying yourself first only works for sure if you create a system that allows you to do to it without having to think about it. When Mark and I began diverting more of each paycheck directly into savings, we noticed that we didn't really miss it. We simply found ways to adapt to the smaller amounts remaining in our checking account. This approach may not work for everyone, but for us, it turns out that artificially constraining our disposable income was the silver bullet to help us save quickly without having to use one bit of will-power to do it. So we decided to take it further, upping the diverted amount even more, increasing our 401(k) contributions to max them out, and eventually adding additional automated investments to our index fund accounts each month. The amount that showed up in our checking account each payday was much less than we were used to, but because that's the only number we saw, that's what we knew was available to spend. And we kept artificially decreasing our income until we really felt it. And that's when we realized that we could actually save so much more than we ever guessed, and not by pinching pennies or clipping coupons, but by gradually shrinking our spending pool and unconsciously finding ways to manage.

The savings side of our approach is hiding money from ourselves, and the spending side is what we think of as our "unbudget." We don't do especially well with traditional line item budgeting, but if we only have so much to spend, we can stick to that. To help you succeed at reaching your goals, consider whether you feel better suited to create a more traditional budget, in which you allocate certain dollars to each item per month, or to artificially constrain your spending, as we did. Either way, you accomplish the same thing, which is minimizing your spending while maximizing how much you can save toward your life goals, so there's no wrong way to do it.

Regardless of which approach you take to managing your spending, there's no downside to hiding money from yourself for savings or investments to avoid the temptation. Here are some things you can do now, and some later as you progress through your journey:

- Set up your payroll to divert part of each paycheck to your high-interest savings account to build up your emergency fund or cash you're saving for other goals like home purchase or rental real estate purchase.
- Set up recurring debt payments well above the minimum payment amount that coincide with payday, so that you only see the extra money in your account for a day or two.
- Consider using services like Qapital or Acorns that operate in the background and automatically round up your purchase amounts and deposit the difference in savings or investment accounts. Your bank may also offer this service.

- Set up automatic monthly investments to your taxable brokerage account. If you get paid twice a month and use a
  large share of the first paycheck to pay rent or the mortgage,
  schedule the automated investment to coincide with the second paycheck, and gradually increase the amount over time,
  especially whenever you get a pay increase or promotion.
- Set up 401(k) contributions through your work plan, and
  periodically increase them if you're finding that you aren't
  feeling squeezed in your spending. Bonus points if you sign
  up for the escalator option that many plans offer to increase
  your contributions by 1 or 2 percentage points at the start of
  each new year, usually coinciding with when you get a pay
  increase, so you won't even notice the difference.

When you create an automated system like this to save, the growth
will feel like magic. (More magic!) You set up the system and then
your only real job is to let time and compounding do their thing. If
you're motivated to save even more, you can gradually increase the
amount you're hiding from yourself via automated investing each
month or every few months until you really feel the pinch in what's
left over to spend. At that point, dial back your investment amounts
slightly to give you some breathing room, and high-five yourself
for finding ways to save even faster by shrinking your comfortable
spending level.

If you can get in the habit as well of banking every windfall you
receive, whether it's a tax refund or a bonus, and constraining your
spending at a constant level despite earning more, your goal money
will balloon and your savings rate will increase exponentially over
time without it feeling like you're doing any additional work or sacrificing things you enjoy. You're just living your life while your investments snowball in the background. That's seriously the closest thing
to magic that I know.

MASSIVE INCREASES IN AVAILABLE GOAL MONEY WITH CONSTRAINED SPENDING

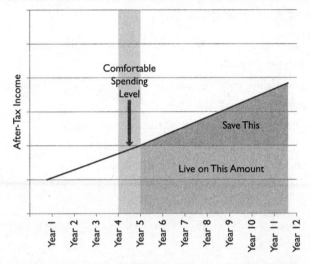

As you're crafting systems to help you succeed, it's easy to get caught up in what is the absolute most optimal solution, but remember that the best system is one you'll actually stick to, not necessarily what's best on paper. For example, a lot of financial experts will scold you if you get a tax refund, because it's like you've given the government an interest-free loan. But here's the thing: If you know you'd just spend that money if you got it in your paycheck and will have an easier time saving it if it comes to you in one big chunk as a refund, then you're doing what's optimal *for you*. Far too much financial advice ignores the reality of human nature, and the best thing you can do to set yourself up to succeed is to not try to pretend you're someone you're not. If I was trying to become someone who could save through sheer force of will alone, I'd still be years from early retirement. By acknowledging that I do best hiding money from myself and not even giving myself the option of spending it, I reached a huge financial goal at an early age. Optimal is only optimal if it truly works for you, and there's no shame in creating your own systems that suit who you are.

FINANCIAL ROADMAP CHECKLIST

☐ Develop a system for tracking your spending and track it for three months.

☐ Determine your comfortable spending level and your current goal money available.

☐ Determine your projected future spending (x).

☐ Determine future expenses you wish to save for, such as children's college or support for aging parents.

☐ Calculate your magic number for whichever version of early retirement you're envisioning.

☐ Create your savings priority sequence, factoring in debt payoff as necessary.

☐ Determine possible future savings increase opportunities, such as a raise or promotion.

☐ Calculate your timeline to early retirement.

☐ Create annual savings milestones to aim for that divide your big goal into smaller chunks.

☐ Create your full early retirement plan spreadsheet (visit TheWorkOptionalBook.com for templates).

☐ Put automated savings and investment systems into place or accelerate debt payoff.

☐ Ratchet up the amount you're saving or investing automatically each month until you find your lowest comfortable spending level.

CHAPTER 8

Accelerate Your Progress

Never stop investing. Never stop improving.
—BOB PARSONS

Let's pause, take a deep breath, and recognize that you've gotten through all of the hardest parts in creating a work-optional life. High five! As a reward for that, I have some more good news: There's an excellent chance you can reach your goal even sooner than your plan suggests. I've met and interviewed dozens of early retirees to date, and the clear trend is that nearly all of them ultimately got to their goal sooner than they originally expected, just like how our 10-year plan gradually morphed into a 6-year plan. An incredible thing happens: After you have your big life vision and roadmap in place, you find that many of your priorities change in ways that help you get to your goals faster.

If you'd asked Mark and me 10 years before retiring if we would be willing to go out to restaurants less, we would have looked at you funny and asked if you knew us at all. We consider experiencing new foods to be a major source of joy in life, and we've often planned entire trips around the restaurants we wanted to try, with visits to museums and cultural sites crammed in awkwardly between meals. We've never paid to take a trip to Disney World, but we did once spend $1,000 on a single meal. (It was Per Se in New York, and though it cost an eye-watering amount, it was worth every penny and we don't regret it. But we also won't be repeating that experience.) That's how important dining was to us: We'd drive a little old car and rarely buy clothes, but drop an embarrassing sum on a single dinner. Now, however, our dining habits are dramatically different. We dine out less, and when we travel, we seek out the best street foods instead of making reservations at the most renowned fine dining establishments. What changed?

After we realized early retirement was possible for us, the vision we shared of a life in the mountains made us feel so fired up that it became miraculously easy to stop spending or reduce our spending without it ever feeling like a sacrifice. We saw that first with the expenditures that we cared much less about. Like no more cable TV. Gone. No more home renovations. Easy. (These things are not unrelated. Getting rid of HGTV reduces home renovation envy big-time.) But even with dining, one of our top priorities, we gradually figured out that what we loved about going out to eat was seeing and tasting the artfully created food, and enjoying the ambiance of beautifully designed spaces, and we finally understood that we didn't need a three-course meal to feel like we'd had a memorable experience. We could dine out much less often and each get an appetizer and single glass of wine, or maybe share an entrée, rather than ordering multiple courses and drinks each. We'd get the experience without delaying our progress toward the thing we wanted most of all. And by doing it less, each occasion felt more special. That's just one example of how our priorities changed after we saw what was possible if we saved more of our money. Saying no becomes so much easier. And continuing to trim your spending is just one way to accelerate your progress. There are a number of other ways you can speed things up and create support structures for yourself to stay on the path. Here are a few.

Boosting Your Income

There are two sides to the saving equation that affect how quickly you can save: how much you earn and how much you spend. And while most of us can reduce what we spend, perhaps by a lot, the potential reduction there is finite. There's a baseline amount that you require to live comfortably. You can't always cut more from your spending, but you can always earn more. As we saw in chapter 7, earning more and banking your increased earnings in your investments is the absolute best way to increase how much you can invest year over year.

There are several big ways you can increase your income: by starting a lucrative side hustle, by retraining for a higher-paying career, by increasing your focus in your current career, by negotiating for more money, or by going to work for yourself.

Work a Side Hustle

Side hustles have grown more common in recent years as younger people especially find them necessary to make ends meet with their student loan debt burdens and high rents in big cities. But side hustles can work for anyone who wants to earn more, assuming you choose one that's truly lucrative. Quite a few multilevel marketing schemes out there prey on folks who are eager to make a little extra on the side, and they often result in those people losing money. A good rule to follow: If you're spending large amounts of money upfront or to keep it going, it's probably not helping you reach your goals.

For 10 years, I taught yoga and spin classes as my side hustle. The startup costs were minimal—a few hundred dollars for my basic certification—and there were almost no ongoing costs. Though I didn't always love having to get up at five a.m. to teach classes, the pay rate was good, and the bonus was that I got paid to work out. Teaching yoga at studios is not always profitable, as there are high costs associated with traditional teacher training, and studios don't all pay fairly, but teaching regular fitness classes at the gym can be a great side hustle.

In general, part-time jobs on top of your full-time job start providing income the fastest, though the income itself may not be huge. If you have the entrepreneurial itch, you could start your own online business that you run in addition to your primary job, though you may have startup costs, and it may take longer to turn a profit. If you're comfortable with that, starting your own business could come with a much higher reward and could continue to provide you with income in early retirement—there's just more risk. Hobby-based businesses like selling homemade crafts on Etsy are an attractive option because they allow you to profit off doing something you enjoy anyway, but make sure your products actually have an audience willing to pay for them before shelling out a bunch of cash for materials.

If you aren't interested in the risks or startup costs of entrepreneurship but do want to have total control over your schedule, there are a range of online options for making additional money, like freelance writing or design, becoming a virtual assistant, and an ever-expanding list of possible other side hustles. The challenge with many of these gigs is the extremely low pay, so before you start promising clients projects that take a ton of your time for all of $5, make sure that you decide how much your time is worth and price your services accordingly.

Retrain for a Higher Paying Career

If the work you're doing currently has an earnings cap that you know will slow your progress toward your early retirement goals, you might consider getting qualified to take on a higher-paying position in another field. Careers in tech and health care in particular are in high demand all over the country and tend to pay well above average, but if there's another career path out there that interests you and pays well, you might find that transitioning into it from where you are is less onerous than many people imagine.

Robin Charlton and her husband, Robert, were highly motivated to save for early retirement, but her low-earning career as a travel agent was holding them back. Rather than settle for a multidecade savings plan, Robin decided to retrain to become a nurse. The accelerated training program took just over a year, and even though it required her to stop working during that period of time, in the long run it paid off. She quickly more than doubled her earnings when she got a nursing job. By boosting their joint income, Robin's decision to retrain helped them shave years off their savings plan, retiring in their early 40s after 12 years of focused investing, even though they earned under six figures combined for most of that time.

A good place to start is to look at regional pay in your area across industries on sites like Glassdoor, identify a few that spark your interest, and then look at the minimum requirements in job listings in those fields. Armed with that information, you can then research programs available online and in your area that would give you the skills and credentials needed to make that career shift. If you feel anxious about investing in training or education broadly, reach out to some local employers and ask for informational interviews. If they accept your request, it's likely because they always need qualified staff, and that's promising. During the conversation, ask them what skills and credentials they look for, and then start doing your homework on how to get that training. Finally, before embarking on new classes, investigate whether your current employer offers any tuition assistance or other benefits that could reduce your out-of-pocket costs.

Some of the most highly paid career paths, based on 2016 median wage data, that require the least education and training include:[1]

- Air-traffic controller ($122,410, requires an associate's degree)
- Nuclear power reactor operator ($91,170, requires a high school diploma)
- Transportation and distribution managers ($89,190, requires a high school diploma)
- Police and detective supervisors ($84,840, requires a high school diploma in many states)
- Power distributors and dispatchers ($81,900, requires a high school diploma)
- Radiation therapist ($80,160, requires an associate's degree)

In addition, many health care careers, such as diagnostic medical sonographer, can earn high five figures with only a certificate program, and disruptions in industries, such as software development by companies like Codecademy, remove traditional institutional barriers to entry and allow you to gain high-demand skills at very little cost.

If you already have a college degree and are looking to boost your income through the retraining method, explore high-paying industries in your area and consider enrolling in a graduate school or certificate program that will qualify you to move into those fields, being mindful not to incur an unmanageable amount of debt to gain these credentials. Do the math to ensure you'll make more in your new field, potentially over a shortened career, to justify the cost.

Just because you started working in one field doesn't mean you're stuck there forever, and if the current path you're on doesn't have good potential to increase your earnings, get creative in looking around at what else you might do and the training you need to do it.

Increase Your Focus in Your Current Career

Though it was a tough balancing act, I managed to teach six to eight spinning and yoga classes a week for 10 years of my career. I was up at five a.m. several days a week to lead early morning rides, and I gave up big chunks of each weekend to guide Angelenos through their sun salutations. I yawned my way through plenty of meetings at work with all the sleep I missed out on, but I loved those classes and the people who came to them. Plus, teaching boosted my income and helped me pay off my debt and later save faster for our home purchases. But eventually, as I took on more responsibility at work, I was having to travel several times a month and was subbing out more and more of my classes. And getting to evening classes was becoming more challenging, as expectations increased that I'd be available to my work clients around the clock. I'd often be rushing to get off a late call and then sprinting to class. It didn't feel good to bluster into class like that, and I knew it wasn't sustainable anymore. So as hard as it was to close that chapter, I realized that giving up my side hustle would allow me to increase my focus and effort at work, which set me up for a promotion, higher pay, and increased opportunities.

Around the same time, Mark decided to increase his focus at work, too. Though he never had a side hustle and had always produced high-quality work that made him beloved by clients and colleagues alike, he'd never really committed to drumming up new business. It was his least favorite part of the job, and he'd always felt uncomfortable stepping into the salesperson role. But he made up his mind that he wanted to demonstrate his commitment to all aspects of his career and stepped outside of his comfort zone to make new business a new priority. In short order, he was earning more and achieved a promotion to his company's highest level, both of which certainly sped our progress toward our savings goal.

You might find that the same approach works for you. Sometimes all that you need to do to earn more is show your current employers that you're redoubling your commitment and effort. It's easy to fall into a pattern of checking out at work as an aspiring early retiree, because you know you won't be in your career forever. But this is the worst thing you can do, both because it makes your days drag by and increases your work stress, and because it puts the brakes on your advancement and earnings potential. If you see your working days as something in short supply and treat them as precious, they truly do become more enjoyable, and it's easier to do the hard work that you need to do to accelerate your progress.

Start by looking around at what opportunities exist at your company, and talk to your supervisor about your desire to move up or earn more, while emphasizing your commitment to the work and the organization. (Make sure you mean it! You don't have to promise to be there for a decade or more, but just to give the work your all for a few years.) Share your ideas for what that could look like, and ask for their input. Depending on your industry, setting some metrics could make sense, agreeing that if you achieve certain milestones it will result in a raise, bonus, or promotion. Think creatively here. Working with more focus doesn't always mean working a whole lot more—it could mean volunteering for a project that no one else wants to take, supervising more people, or solving a problem the company didn't know it had. For me, it meant saying yes to more travel, and though it kept me away from home more, a lot of that travel was fun. Increasing your focus at work might very well mean working more, but don't go in assuming that. If early retirement is something that you want that badly, working more for a limited period of time might feel worthwhile.

Negotiate for More—at the Same Job or Elsewhere

Negotiating for pay is becoming more acceptable, but it's worth remembering that you haven't missed the boat if you didn't negotiate for pay coming into your current job. If you work hard and are a valued employee, employers want to keep you happy. Employee turnover is extremely costly to employers, so they want to keep you, period. And if you can make the case diplomatically for why you believe you deserve more, you may find that you'll get it.

Make the conversation collegial instead of confrontational, come prepared with regional pay data from Glassdoor and local job listings, and say that you'd like to discuss your compensation. It might simply be enough to say that you believe you've earned a raise. Or you might need to provide a recap of your accomplishments, including the ones that aren't top of mind for your supervisor. And you might need to bust out those pay stats for your industry and region. A strong negotiating tactic is to tell your supervisor that you'd like a raise and wish to discuss what it would take to earn it. Agree together upon specific, measurable goals you will work toward, and after the meeting, really work toward them. Four to six weeks later, go back to your supervisor with specific examples of where you've improved as agreed or of higher level work you've taken on to demonstrate that you've followed through on your promise. And then ask for your compensation to be increased accordingly. The decision of whether to increase your pay is ultimately up to your employer, and not everyone will welcome having this conversation. But by keeping it friendly and nonconfrontational at each step of the negotiation, you minimize the chance that asking for more could backfire. And it very well may be successful.

Of course, if you're changing jobs, you have a big opportunity. When you receive a job offer, that's your time to make the case for why you may be worth more to that employer than they are offering you. Again, look at industry and local pay data, look at your own salary history if it helps you (but don't feel chained to it if it doesn't—many states now prohibit employers from asking for your salary history in an effort to avoid perpetuating gender- and race-based wage gaps). Let the employer know that you're excited about the opportunity but wish to discuss the compensation. There are many books devoted to negotiation techniques, but the most basic approaches are to ask if that's their best offer, throw out a counteroffer, or play multiple offers off one another to see if either party will sweeten the deal. If they won't budge on salary, explore whether they might consider building incentives into your pay structure if you achieve certain targets that make sense in the job or if you stay a certain amount of time. The impact of a one-time pay bump that is then compounded by annual increases can be enormous over the course of an entire career. For example, negotiating 5% more on top of a $45,000 salary at age 24 would result in a cumulative earnings difference of $53,319 by age 40, $105,939 by age 50, and a whopping $235,844 by age 65 compared to someone who didn't negotiate the raise. Of course, this is assuming 4% annual raises (slightly above average, but no additional promotions, which would magnify the difference even more). You're not just negotiating for the extra $2,250 that 5% would come out to in that first year; you're negotiating for how that difference compounds over time. Remember: Everything compounds. If you push a little more and negotiate a single 10% raise, the difference is even more dramatic: $106,639 by age 40, $211,879 by 50, and $471,688 by 65. All that from a difference of $4,500 early in your career. That said, 10–20% pay increases are uncommon within the same job in most fields, so if you're serious about increasing your income, your best bet may be to change jobs and negotiate seriously before accepting a new offer.

Go to Work for Yourself

If you're willing to take the risk that comes from forgoing a regular paycheck, the quickest way to accelerate your progress may be to start your own full-time business. Stanley and Danko's research shows that a high percentage of people who achieve $1 million net worth own their own small businesses. And we're not talking about high-value tech startups. We're talking about auto repair shops, dry cleaners, accounting businesses—not the glamorous jobs you may be picturing. Particularly if you are in a two-income household and one partner has a secure job that will cover your expenses easily, it may be worth your while for the other partner to strike out on their own. As a small business owner you get to keep a larger share of the revenue you generate than you do when working for someone else, and you can control your overhead expenses. Self-employed people also enjoy special tax advantages that especially benefit early retirees, including the ability to save much more in tax-advantaged retirement accounts like a solo 401(k). Of course, this option likely won't appeal to you if you're generally financially risk-averse, and there's no shame in keeping your focus on maximizing your income through traditional employment. Mark and I contemplated starting our own small consulting business, but ultimately decided that wasn't worth all the extra legwork and stress given how few years we planned to keep working full-time, and we decided to stay in the jobs we ultimately retired from.

Reducing Spending on the Largest Expenses

When I was 22, working an entry-level job and living in Washington, DC, I remember reading a profile in the *Washington Post* of a young couple who'd managed to save to buy a home in that expensive market. They'd done it by never going out to eat and eating rice and beans almost every day, and I remember thinking, *That sounds so joyless. I guess I'm not cut out to save money.* It turns out, of course, that I was cut out to save money, but not by subsisting on rice and beans. So let me assure you: I am not going to tell you to eat rice and beans for every meal, to buy only foods for which you have coupons, or to give up lattes if you truly savor them. Wanting some variety in your meals does not mean that you're not cut out to save money. That's only one possible way to save, and you'll get more bang for your buck if you focus on the largest expenses first and give up only the little stuff that no longer feels worth it to you, rather than wasting time and mental energy trying to pinch every possible penny. The bulk of most people's income goes to two things: housing and transportation. So start there.

Reduce Your Housing Costs

You've already asked yourself what's most important to you in life and what you need to be happy, so you probably already know the answer to the question: Could you decrease your housing costs? If you love your home and can't picture your life anywhere else, no problem. In that case, focus on other ways to accelerate your progress. But if you could imagine downsizing, moving to a less expensive area, getting a roommate, or renting your home out on the weekends on Airbnb, then you have options to speed yourself along. If you own your home, you could even rent it out and use part of that income to rent a smaller home for yourself—just note that net rental income is taxable, so factor in income taxes before deciding whether this makes sense for you.

I talked in chapter 5 about our thought process in setting our housing budget when we moved from Los Angeles to Tahoe. That year, home prices in Tahoe were down as much as 50% from the peak in 2007, it was a buyer's market, and interest rates were at historic lows. It was the absolute best time to buy, and we couldn't believe our luck in being ready then. Knowing that our dollar would go much further at that time than after prices recovered, we could have easily justified why it was okay to spend more. Mark still sometimes jokingly laments that we didn't buy the much more expensive "blue-roof house" with the spectacular view, but we both know that setting our own budget that was lower than what the banks said our budget should be was the single best financial decision we ever made. If we'd spent more, we wouldn't have been able to pay off our mortgage in under six years, and we'd almost certainly still be working instead of having retired early.

Even before we bought our house, our single best money hack has always been underspending on housing. We may have been spending obscene sums on dinners out and travel, but we did so while living in a dingy one-bedroom apartment in West Hollywood that we rented for years, even though our earnings increased and we knew we could afford to move if we wanted to. Much of the decision to stay was pure laziness and the fact that we loved our location. But we still saved a ton of money by not moving, and looking back, we're thrilled that we accidentally made a great financial decision.

Of course, there are also those who are perfectly happy going for an even more extreme option. Steve and Courtney Adcock knew they wanted to retire early, but their number crunching told them it was still going to take several years at their current spending and income levels. They owned two houses in Tucson, Arizona, one of which they rented out, but they'd bought during the absolute peak of the market in 2007. Their mortgage payments were so large that they were slowing their savings progress. They made the unconventional decision to give up living in a house altogether, sold both of their homes, bought an Airstream travel trailer, and set off for a nomadic lifestyle—or, as they put it, taking their home with them wherever they go. Having a permanent home base isn't part of what they need to be happy, and so changing their living arrangement allowed them to reduce their living expenses, which reduced the amount they needed to save and let them retire in their mid-30s.

It's your call what might be right for you, but if you are game to reduce your housing expenses, you may free up hundreds of dollars a month in an instant, and you can funnel that newfound cash into your investments. No amount of couponing or thrift store shopping will give you such a big savings boost all in one shot, so question your housing expenses before you nickel-and-dime the rest of your budget.

Trim Your Transportation Spending

After housing, transportation is the next biggest expense in most households, and there are a lot of ways to save here that might work for you. The most basic question to ask is whether you need a car or, if you're a multicar household, if you need as many as you have. Even a paid-off car comes with ownership costs of several thousand dollars a year from insurance, gas, maintenance, and parking. If you are making payments on that car or, worse, leasing it, then add several thousand more dollars per year. Going carless is not an option for everyone, but if you live in a walkable area or a city with good public transportation, you might find that ridesharing and car-sharing services provide all the car time you need. If having a car is critical, consider ways to reduce your costs: keeping one car for a long time instead of upgrading, buying instead of leasing, buying used, increasing your insurance deductible to drop your premium, or just driving less to save gas.

We're still a two-car household, and we bought both of our cars new, so you need not go carless or only buy used, high-mileage cars to be able to retire early. But we did buy economical, reliable cars (a 2004 Honda Civic and a 2012 Subaru Outback), and we negotiated the heck out of the prices by emailing the fleet department at multiple dealerships asking for their best price on the car with the specs we wanted, and then sharing the lowest of those bids with all the dealers again, asking them to beat it, and repeating the process until we were confident we had the lowest possible price. In addition, we paid cash for the Outback, which saved us the interest charges of an auto loan, and we'll keep both cars until they die. Sure, our friends and colleagues in LA might have been driving BMWs and Audis while we pulled up in our modest little Honda, but knowing that trading up for a more expensive or newer car would mean having to work longer made it easier to shrug off any self-consciousness about our ride.

The conundrum for many people is that housing and transportation often have an inverse relationship. You can live closer to the urban center and pay less for transportation but more for housing, or you can live in the suburbs where homes cost less but where you have to drive more. Taking a look at prices in your area, you might find that you can save enough in transportation costs to make it worth moving closer to the city center and paying more to live there, or vice versa. Before he and his wife, Winnie Tseng, retired in their 30s, Jeremy Jacobson was spending a fortune in transportation, commuting to his job at Microsoft in Seattle. By moving to a smaller place closer to work, he was able to stop spending money on transportation altogether, and to walk or bike everywhere. Even though housing typically costs more in the urban core, he was willing to downsize his space so dramatically that his housing costs decreased on top of eliminating all transportation costs. His savings rate skyrocketed, and he and Winnie now travel the world with their young son.

Other High-Impact Ways to Trim Spending

There are a lot of ways to spend less money, but some of them take so much effort that they actively detract from your quality of life. I spent a year couponing aggressively, and looking back, it was a colossal waste of time, not to mention it drove us to buy unhealthy junk food instead of fresh healthy food, for which there are no coupons. I'd love to get back the time that I spent tracking down the best coupon deals and arguing with cashiers about stores' double coupon policies, but at least it taught me a valuable lesson: It's far better to focus on the savings techniques that aren't too onerous and suit your temperament, and give up the rest. In other words: Play to your strengths.

For example, some people genuinely love thrift store shopping. They love the thrill of the hunt and the joy of finding the perfect piece for a huge discount. That's not me. I quickly get overwhelmed and headachy when I try to shop at thrift stores, and for years, I felt guilty about buying my clothing items new, because I knew I could be paying less. I realized, though, that there were things I was well suited for that some of my thrift-shopping friends weren't, like taking on some of the dirtier home maintenance and DIY projects and negotiating for the best deals when we do need to hire things out. How I feel about thrift shopping is how they feel about negotiations, and so we each do what suits us to reduce our spending. What are the ways you actually enjoy saving money, versus the ones that feel like more trouble than they're worth? Put your energy there.

Beyond housing and transportation, look at what your biggest expenses are. Is it dining out, like it was for us? An expensive hobby? New clothes? Nonessential spending on kids? Ask yourself the question we did when we concluded that we didn't need three courses to enjoy a dining experience: *What is really the core element that you love and can't live without?* If you love to travel, there's a lot that goes into that, not all of which is a necessity. Do you love staying in a nice hotel, or do you not care where you sleep so long as you are in a new and interesting place? Do you care whether you do expensive activities when you get to a new city or country, or do you really just love walking around and soaking up the culture? For the big expenses that you love and value most, get granular to figure out if you can still get the essence of the experience while spending much less.

Hacking Your Way to Cheaper Travel

Pursuing an early retirement goal asks you to reduce both what you're spending in the accumulation phase to boost your savings rate and what you'll spend in the future so that you don't need to save many millions of dollars to afford your lifestyle. And if you wish to prioritize travel despite trimming your spending significantly, travel hacking may appeal to you. Travel hacking is being strategic about maximizing travel credit card sign-up bonuses and using those points to fund your travel rather than using your own cash, and when combined with off-peak travel to avoid paying the rates of high seasons and weekends, many travel hackers spend very little on their trips. Credit card companies will offer new customers with strong credit scores some number of travel miles or points if they meet a minimum spending requirement, for example, enough points to pay for a round-trip flight to Europe if you spend $3,000 in the first three months the card is open. If you charge everything you spend on the card and then pay it off right away, you can accrue points or miles without spending any new money. You can travel hack as much or as little as you like, from signing up for maybe just one new card a year to churning multiple cards at a time.

I've always found the idea of keeping track of many credit cards, their spending requirements, and their billing deadlines too stressful, so we've only signed up for one to two new cards a year, but we've netted several hundred thousand travel points that way. (And so long as you have good credit to begin with and make your payments on time, signing up for a few new cards a year won't drag down your credit score by more than a few digits, though some banks like Chase have rules limiting how many new cards you can be approved for in a given period.) Those points were worth a few thousand dollars, and we didn't spend anything beyond our normal expenses and a few annual fees. Even if you don't want to travel hack, it's still worth considering using a travel points credit card so you can earn points from your regular spending. And if you travel for work, investigate whether it's possible to keep your miles for personal use, and aim to fly and stay with only one or two airlines and hotel chains to increase the likelihood of earning enough points to convert to free travel. Of course, all of these tips only apply if you trust yourself to use credit cards responsibly and you pay off your balance in full each month. If you currently have credit card debt or worry that you might run up a balance, rest assured that the benefits of paying off your debt or staying debt-free far outweigh the benefits of travel hacking.

In the simplest terms, if you focus only on four primary steps, none of which require you to pinch pennies, you'll find that you make fast progress toward your financial goal. The more you can maximize each one, the more you'll accelerate your pace.

Formula for fast savings progress:

1. Underspend on housing
2. Underspend on transportation
3. Focus on increasing your earnings
4. Bank your raises, increasing your savings rate to match your increased earnings

As with everything money-related, there are the purely financial aspects, and then there are the feelings that go along with them. We've just gone through the financial strategies for accelerating your progress, and now we'll look at the emotional side.

Accelerating Your Progress Mentally and Emotionally

After you've learned the financial principles of early retirement and put your systems into place, money becomes the easy part. The hard part is everything else: all the tough questions you must ask yourself to envision the life you want to work toward, figuring out what you're willing to change, and—most of all—waiting it out. When you craft your early retirement financial plan, you'll get a handle on your finances, you'll get busy saving, and then...you'll wait. For most people, the timeline to early retirement is at least a handful of years, or it might be a decade or more. And while that's super fast compared to the vast majority of Americans' progress toward retirement, there's no point in denying that we're talking about years. In that time, it's natural to get impatient. It's also natural to feel some stress from the process if you don't have social support for what might look like a pretty major lifestyle shift. Fortunately, if you know that impatience and lack of support are the nonfinancial barriers that can arise on your journey, you can take steps to head them off, just as you can take steps to remove temptations that might make it hard to stick to your plan and to practice self-care to cope with work stress and keep you moving down the path.

- **Conquer impatience:** Nearly everyone we know who achieved early retirement hit a patch of impatience or two while in the savings phase. It absolutely happened to us. In our case, the impatience grew out of a feeling of burnout at work, something that plenty of people who aren't saving for early retirement experience. And it's possible that our secret plans actually exacerbated our feeling of burnout, because we felt so close to being able to retire instead of having to survive our jobs like most people. The experience taught us a lot, though, and we found some excellent ways to tamp down impatience whenever those feelings started bubbling up, as well as to head it off in the first place.
- **Celebrate intermediate milestones:** Chances are that you'll be focused on saving a large amount, whatever you deem your magic number. But that number isn't the only one worth celebrating. Choose some intermediate milestones along the way—maybe many of them—and celebrate them for real. We splurged on a celebratory ski trip after we paid off our mortgage, and we popped a nice bottle of Champagne each time we hit a new $100,000 increment in our net worth. We high-fived for many more small milestones along the way. In the last few years of saving, it felt like we were celebrating a mini milestone every few months, which kept us focused on the progress we were making, rather than how far we still had left to go.
- **Institute a work complaint ban:** Impatience seems most likely to arise when work is the busiest or most stressful.

And it's in those moments when it's easy to get into a downward spiral of feeling sorry for ourselves for the very fact that we have to work and aren't retired yet. This can be harmful to your mental state, but it also detracts from the whole journey to early retirement because it makes you forget how lucky and fortunate you are to be able to pursue early retirement at all. For us, nothing made the journey feel faster than when we instituted a rule that we weren't allowed to complain about work. We could recount things that had happened at work, but we weren't allowed to complain about the fact that we had to work or about things that would be common and expected in any job. That ban helped us remember that being able to work is a privilege in itself, and it made us more appreciative of the good parts of our own jobs. But most of all, we realized that when we complained about work, the journey felt like a slog, and when we didn't, it passed much more quickly and easily.

- **Focus on the best parts of work:** Every job has aspects of it that no one wants to do. (If it didn't, why would they pay you to do it?) But you can choose whether you want to focus on the stuff you don't like or focus on the best parts. Ask yourself: What are the parts of work that you enjoy doing and might even miss? It might be a particular task that you are especially good at, something you get to learn about, or interaction with coworkers you respect or like. If nothing comes to mind immediately, there's a good chance that your mind is tricking you into thinking that all of your job is bad just because part of it is bad. This is rarely true, so challenge yourself to dig a little deeper. Think about everything you have the opportunity to learn, every task you do, and every person in your work orbit. Think about when you get asked for your opinion or feel valued for your contributions.

Chances are good you'll find several big positives that are worth focusing on. When I started thinking about work this way, I quickly realized that not only did I love giving presentations and being asked for my opinion in challenging situations, but I would actually miss those things after we retired early. And that drove me to think of ways I could incorporate presenting and solving challenges into my early retirement, so that I didn't have to give those things up entirely. But more importantly, focusing on how much I enjoyed those things made me look forward to work more and it helped me brush off the stuff I didn't enjoy as much. Thinking this way even made it a little hard to leave work when we were ready financially.

- **Try nostalgia in advance:** There's no shame in employing a few little mental tricks like "nostalgia in advance" if they help you get through a situation. During my last few years of work, whenever I'd do a presentation, I'd remind myself beforehand that this was something I'd miss a lot after we quit, and I'd pour my whole heart and soul into that session. I'm positive that this made my presentations better for those who saw them, but it also made them more meaningful to me. That's a positive example, but when nostalgia in advance really works well is in the less pleasant instances. In those meetings that got tense, I'd tell myself, *One day I'll look back at this and chuckle*, and that thought alone would instantly make me feel more calm. In essence, I'd imagine my future self looking back at those tough work memories and let that feeling replace the stress in the moment. It sounds wacky, but it works.

- **Practice gratitude:** When none of those tricks work, the best antidote to impatience is simply reminding yourself how few people in history have ever been able to achieve true financial security, let alone a work-optional life. (Even fabulously wealthy royalty still have to work!) Those of us in the early retirement movement are truly some of the luckiest people who've ever lived, and remembering that never ceases to make us feel enormously grateful.

Building Strong Social Support

Saving for early retirement is a big deal. It may completely reshape how you wish to spend your money and therefore the types of activities that you find worthwhile. While many people in your life will support you in your goals, unconventional as they are, it's possible that you'll get some pushback. The positive kind of pushback is from those who are simply concerned for you; because early retirement is not yet a mainstream idea, they just haven't seen the math laid out for them and therefore worry that you might run out of money. Breaking some of the concepts down for them will likely bring them around so that they can cheer you on in your journey.

The bigger concern is the folks whose support doesn't come naturally, and with some of them, you may find that once you no longer spend money on something you both did together, you have nothing in common and start drifting apart. That's fine. It's a problem when you find that most people in your life are critical of your new life choices or, worse, that your new lifestyle leaves you with no social support structure. Here's how you can ensure those challenges don't derail your progress.

- **Create social circles with aligned spending habits:** If you are accustomed to spending one way and make big changes as a part of your early retirement plan, that could have a ripple effect in your social circles. For example, when we lived in LA, seeing friends meant going out to dinner that could easily cost $100 or more. When we decided that we would rather save that money than spend it, we realized that that might mean finding some new friends who were game to have a picnic in the park instead or to get coffee rather than dinner and drinks. In our case, this realization coincided with our move to Tahoe, but we made a conscious effort to find new friends who were more eager to do free activities like going for a hike rather than dropping big bucks on a night out.

- **Choose your words wisely:** It's helpful to have a phrase at the ready that you can toss out whenever someone wants you to spend money you'd rather save instead. "I can't afford it" is the default for most folks, but for people who know your plans and that you're saving deliberately, that might cause more trouble than it's worth, with people wishing to litigate what *afford* means and whether you're telling the truth. Kids might be the toughest critics of that line. Do yourself the favor of not having to revisit this question multiple times and choose a phrase that shuts the conversation down more efficiently. It could be "That's not in the budget," "That's not a priority for us," "Spending less will give us more time together as a family," or something more pointed like "That would slow my progress." We went with a more simple phrase that was quite effective at ending the discussion: "We're not going to be able to do that right now."

- **Look online:** It undoubtedly sped our progress to early retirement to have an online network of friends with similar goals. If you happen to have friends in real life who are pursuing financial independence or early retirement, count yourself lucky. But for all the rest of us, online support can fill that void. If you feel inspired, starting an early retirement blog will bring more potential online friends to you, but be aware that blogging is hard, time-consuming work that's best suited to those who love writing and would do it even without a blog. Fortunately, even if you don't blog, you can comment on other people's blog posts and strike up friendships that way. Don't let the fact that most other commenters are bloggers stop you—if you express genuine interest in blogs you connect with, and then maybe progress to emailing directly or connecting on social media, you may find that you have some very real friendships in your life in no time. Another avenue to explore is local financial independence meetups, which are starting to pop up all over the world. Search for groups focused on early retirement; financial independence (FI); and financial independence, retire early (FIRE).

- **Keep your eyes on the prize:** If all else fails and people in your life are pressuring you to spend money on their priorities instead of your own, remind yourself as often as you need to why you're doing all of this. To give yourself more time to pursue your passions. To be more present with a partner or your kids. To see the world. That urge to keep up with the Joneses can be powerful for others, but you'll be less likely to be swayed if you keep your own carefully crafted money mission statement and life vision front and center in your mind.

Practicing Self-Care on Your Journey

In addition to feeling impatient at times along the way or wondering if you're crazy for wanting something so unconventional for your life, you will also likely feel the totally normal effects of work that nearly everyone feels these days: stress, exhaustion, even burnout. If you're serious about reaching your early retirement savings goals, you need to take good care of yourself so that you can keep going until you've hit your magic number. Develop coping techniques to deal with your work stress, whether that's making time for yoga or taking walks during your work breaks, and then prioritize them. Use all your vacation time, and don't make the mistake we made in our last couple of years of work, thinking that if we worked more, we'd earn more. It's possible we did, but we also wore ourselves out. Give yourself those much-needed breaks, and unplug as much as you can while you're on vacation, even if it's just a free staycation at home.

If you used to take a "treat yo'self" attitude to spending to cope with work stress, then add additional supports so that you don't feel totally deprived. Allocate a small fun money allowance that you can spend on anything you want, no matter how frivolous, so that you can still say yes to happy hour or lunch out with colleagues if the opportunity arises. And keep working toward near-term fun goals, too, like taking a trip you're looking forward to or making a small update to your home that will improve its comfort. If you feel like you're deferring all joy until some future date, you'll find it much harder to stick to your plan, but if you allow yourself fun along the way, you can keep making fast progress so long as those splurges don't get out of hand.

JOURNEY ACCELERATION CHECKLIST

- ☐ Determine whether you'd like to try to earn more and, if so, how you'll go about it.
- ☐ Negotiate a higher salary or rate where possible.
- ☐ Investigate side hustles or retraining opportunities.

☐ Look for ways to cut large costs like housing and transportation.
☐ Trim travel spending through travel hacking.
☐ Build social networks for support in your journey.
☐ Practice regular self-care.

CHAPTER 9

Make Your Plan Bulletproof

There are risks and costs to action. But they are far less than the long range risks of comfortable inaction.

—JOHN F. KENNEDY

The hardest part of early retirement for me—actually leaving a secure and well-paid career that I enjoyed—was mental: that nagging question, *But what if we run out of money?* The reality is that people who plan for early retirement get much more on top of their finances than the average, but when society teaches us that the "right" way to do things is to work until 65, making the choice to diverge from that prescribed path can feel especially risky, whether it actually is or not. And if you have that nagging concern, too, of whether you'll have enough saved to last your entire lifetime and should reconsider walking away from your career, it's worth digging into ways you can allay that concern. Some folks will toss out the easy answer that you can always just go back to work, but anyone who has struggled to find work in a recession knows that isn't always true. Not to mention that when you'd be most likely to need to go back to work is when stocks are underperforming, which is also when employers tend not to be hiring. Add to that the possibility that you might also have a sizeable resume gap to contend with, or you may have reached an age that makes it hard to go back to work, and it makes sense not to think of going back to work as your only real fallback option. Plus, why put in all that effort for years to save for early retirement if you might end up back at work anyway out of necessity? It's far better to strengthen your plan and add in some additional safeguards against the unpredictable financial challenges that may come your way. In this chapter, we'll go through the full range of contingencies you can build into your plan so that running out of money is something you never worry about again.

Diversify Your Magic Money Sources

Though economic forces are all connected, and periods of recession will tend to depress stock prices, home prices, and jobs jointly, there are many cases in which economic forces tend to work inversely. For example, when stock markets are down, bond values tend to rise as investors seek out more stable assets. When housing prices increase in big cities, that sometimes means housing prices drop in small towns and rural areas, as people leave those places for the better economic opportunities in the urban areas. You want to ensure that you're not too heavily invested in one sector, asset class, or geographic region, so that you aren't tying your livelihood to too small a slice of the economy as a whole. That means diversifying your magic money–generating assets, whether you're investing in the markets or real estate.

If you choose to invest in index funds, they are automatically diversified for you. If you wish to be even more diversified, however, you can look beyond the US at total international stock and bond index funds that give you ownership of a tiny slice of the entire global market, so you can make sure you're well covered, both to capitalize on gains around the world and to insulate against losses in one sector or country. If you're focusing your investing strategy on real estate, it makes sense to diversify your investments to some extent as well. That could be by investing in multiple types of properties, such as both single family homes and multifamily apartment buildings. Or it could be by investing in properties in a few different geographic locations, ideally all of which themselves have diversified job markets and aren't overly reliant on a single large employer or industry. As we've seen in countless small towns and mid-sized cities across the Rust Belt, if a factory closes or an industry moves overseas, a whole region might face serious economic hardship. You don't want to be stuck not being able to find tenants for an extended period and find yourself unable to sell off your properties as a last resort.

Allocate Your Assets to Protect You—and So They Can Grow

Being a successful investor means embracing a bit of a paradox: The assets that seem the safest—like money in a savings account—are actually dangerous in the long run, because they cannot grow enough to protect your purchasing power. And the ones that seem a bit riskier because they can fluctuate in value—like stocks and stock index funds—are most likely to protect you in the long run because they have the greatest potential to increase in value. So protecting yourself really works both ways: insulating yourself against the investments that carry volatility risk by also holding stable assets like bonds, but also not investing so conservatively that you miss out on growth you need to make your money last your full retirement.

That's the importance of asset allocation: to balance both sides of that equation.

The old standard allocation advice was to subtract your age from 100 to determine the percentage of your invested assets that you should have in stocks. So if you're 30 right now, you'd have 70% of your investments in stocks and 30% in bonds. However, people are living longer than ever, and with bond yields down, many experts are recommending that you shift the starting number to 110 or even 120. So if you're 30 now with the new formula, you'd want 80–90% of your portfolio in stocks and only 10–20% in bonds. This high allocation in stocks gives your portfolio more opportunity to grow over the many decades it should have to do so than it would if it was constrained by too high a percentage of bonds, but you'd still have some safety buffer with that small bond allocation.

120 – AGE = PERCENTAGE TO ALLOCATE TO STOCK INDEX FUNDS
(110 – AGE if more conservative)

That said, there are two circumstances when it makes sense to diverge from this advice. First, if you're brand-new to investing, you may feel uncomfortable putting most of your money into volatile assets like stocks. Money is an emotional thing, and it's fine if you need a period with training wheels until you get more accustomed to the feeling of investing. In that case, consider a conservative allocation like this one for the time being, building up your cash funds, stock fund holdings, and bond fund holdings in tandem:

BEGINNING ALLOCATION

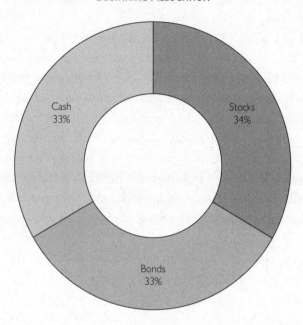

The second circumstance is if you're looking to retire in the next five years or so. In that case, regardless of your age, it makes sense to have a slightly larger bond allocation in addition to a cash buffer, so that you have ample ability to avoid selling stock shares in the event you hit a bad sequence of returns early in your retirement. Retirement advisors recommend that retirees of all ages begin retirement with two to three years' worth of living expenses in cash, preferably in a high-interest savings account. The cash buffer can be the last thing you save as this money will earn you the least interest, so you want to focus first on building up assets that will generate magic money over the long term. But after you've built up enough in your stock funds and bond funds, you can focus on allocating more to cash so that you retire with an allocation in the range of:

110 – AGE = PERCENTAGE IN STOCKS
AGE – 10 = PERCENTAGE IN BONDS AND CASH
COMBINED

Ultimately, there's no answer that's best for everyone universally, but the general age-based guidelines are helpful to ensure you don't go too far in either direction to reach your goals. The Trinity study of safe withdrawal rates found very little difference in long-term outcomes between a range of stock versus bond allocations, assuming portfolios were at least 50% stock, with the withdrawal rate used being the far better predictor of whether a portfolio lasted the entire length of that theoretical retirement. Here again, Monte Carlo simulators like cFIREsim can be extremely useful to check that you're setting yourself up to succeed, and you may find it worthwhile to have a certified financial planner provide a second opinion to check your work.

Create a Strong Withdrawal Strategy

More than just having a truly safe withdrawal rate (SWR), which we talked about in chapter 6, you also need a strategy for withdrawing (drawing down) funds that will maximize the ability of your remaining portfolio to continue growing after you've taken funds out. This is an area retirement economists have studied far less than you'd think, given how much retirement advisors will happily charge you with the promise that they have all the answers. There are several approaches to withdrawing funds from your portfolio to pay for your lifestyle, but some have a greater likelihood of success than others. The most conservative option is to live off only dividends and interest generated by your assets and avoid actually selling shares. While this will guarantee that you do not deplete your principal, it is not an ideal long-term strategy as inflation will erode your purchasing power over time. And as we discussed in chapter 4, investing in dividend stocks might force you to amass a much larger portfolio than you'd need with a drawdown investing approach, meaning you'd have to work and save longer. It is a good idea, however, to switch your account settings from reinvesting dividends to cashing out dividends when you retire, as these dividends count as income for tax and health care premium purposes, and so you're best off including them in your cash flow. Spending your dividends first is a given, regardless of which withdrawal strategy you adopt.

The simplest strategy for selling shares (the drawdown approach) is to sell proportionally: If your portfolio is 80/20 stocks to bonds, you'd sell 80% of the needed dollars from your stock funds and 20% from your bond funds. However, analysis by Darrow Kirkpatrick shows that the best approach by a long shot is not to sell off shares proportionately, but to look at how stocks and bonds are faring against the CAPE median index. Economist Robert Schiller developed the cyclically adjusted price-to-earnings (CAPE) ratio to give investors a clear sense of when stocks and bonds are overvalued and undervalued relative to earnings, and the CAPE median figure tells you which between stocks or bonds is overperforming relative to long-term averages. When you go to make your investment account withdrawals, you'd consult the CAPE median, and if stocks are currently above it, you withdraw from your stock funds. If stocks are currently below the CAPE median, you'd withdraw from bond funds. Though the methodology sounds complicated, all of the complicated math is what goes into the index, so the only thing you need to know is whether stocks are currently above or below the line, which you can see at a glance. You can look up the current CAPE and long-term CAPE median online any time, including at the site listed in this book's "Additional Resources" section. Another way to think about this approach is that by selling stocks when they are highest and selling bonds when stocks are lowest, you are selling the fewest shares at any given time to fund your retirement, which is the best approach for long-term growth and preservation of your principal.

If you have a more complex investment portfolio and it's not simply a matter of selling shares from your few stock index funds, consult the CAPE median first to tell you whether you should sell stocks or bonds generally, and then sell shares from the stocks or funds that have made the highest percentage gains in the last year or quarter, again so that you are selling the fewest shares. The CAPE median approach is certainly not the only way to decide what to draw down from your portfolio, but it's a good option if you like simplicity. Whether you sell shares annually, quarterly, or monthly is up to you, though you may wish to delay your last withdrawal of the year as long as possible so that you can factor in dividends and other income received and calculate how much you'll withdraw in concert with decisions like how much you'll also convert to Roth IRA in that tax year. Many early retirees look to optimize their income specifically to stay within a particular tax bracket or to avoid increasing their health insurance premiums, and waiting until late in the year to make final decisions about withdrawals and Roth contributions may make sense in your situation.

Know How and When to Cut Expenses

If you're concerned that you might be running low on money, the very best thing you can do is spend less. You don't want to plan for a life in which you're technically surviving but not getting to spend money on the things that are meaningful to you, but you also want to be sure that you *could* cut your spending if you had to. So take a look at your spending plan and ask yourself: What could you cut if you needed to tighten your belt by, say, 10% for a year or two? What could you cut if you needed to trim things more dramatically, by 25 or 30%? What's the most you could cut your spending if you absolutely had to, without foregoing any necessities like housing, nutritious food, and health care? Map out what those spending plans look like and file them away in your contingencies folder, as backup plans should you need them. And then, as we discussed regarding sequence risk, if markets are trending downward or flat during your initial early retirement years, you can make the choice to constrain your spending to ensure that you reach the end of your first decade with enough left to sustain you through the remainder of your retirement. There could very well be other ways to achieve the same thing, such as working a little bit more so that you're spending mostly new earnings and leaving your investments alone during especially volatile periods, but it's important to know what you would do in the case that you couldn't find work.

Though for most of us, finding ways to trim expenses to the absolute minimum is our rainy day plan, Bianca DiValerio made it the cornerstone of her early retirement plan, an approach that has her on track to retire in her early 40s despite being single, not having a college degree, and having emerged from divorce and multiple short sales a few years ago with very little saved. She earns $75,000 as a flight attendant, but by focusing on spending the absolute minimum, she saves 75% of that, and side hustles aggressively with dog sitting and refurbishing Craigslist furniture finds to save even more. Some of the measures she has taken to keep her expenses low include living in a studio condo instead of a larger space, in a part of Chicago where it's cheaper to live because it's not thought of as a fancy neighborhood, keeping her purchases to an absolute minimum, and by buying groceries exclusively at discount stores Aldi and Costco. Bianca is a living example of the principle that the less your lifestyle costs, the less you have to save. Her lifestyle may not work for everyone, but she decided that freedom from mandatory work was worth the trade-off of giving up more extravagant expenses.

Build In Backup Sources of Capital

If you're concerned about potentially running out of money one day, the best thing you can do for yourself is to build in actual backup pools of money that you can tap if absolutely necessary. Of course your goal is never to need to, but knowing that you have the option will give you tremendous confidence in your plan.

For homeowners, the biggest potential pool of additional funds is likely your primary residence, and if you were undecided about which way to go with housing earlier, perhaps this discussion will sway you. If you choose a lifetime of renting or of something even more spartan like RV travel, you don't have a built-in backup plan the way that homeowners do. When you own, if you're truly in a bad spot financially, you can always sell your house and use the proceeds of that sale to fund your living expenses for a time. How long that money will last you depends on how much equity you have in your home, how the housing market in your area is faring at that moment, and how much your lifestyle costs. And of course you have to fund new housing somehow, so that's part of the equation. In our case, though we bought far less house than the banks would have lent us, we are not in the smallest house we could see ourselves in and could certainly downsize if we needed to do so to free up some cash. Because we paid off our house, we have 100% equity and could potentially stretch that quite far. If things got even worse than that, we could sell the smaller home and either live in an RV full-time or move to a less expensive part of the country or world where our money would stretch further, so we see our house as a two-layer contingency which gives us a lot of comfort. While I would never recommend living in a larger house than you need just to give yourself a contingency plan, consider whether you could downsize your home or move from your ideal retirement location to a lower-cost-of-living area to free up funds if you truly need to.

Another option for homeowners is to consider opening—but not using—a home equity line of credit (HELOC) before you leave your career. The approval process for a HELOC is similar to getting a mortgage, so it helps enormously to have regular income and is much easier to secure the line of credit while you still have continuous income. If you can find an offer for a HELOC with a low interest rate, low origination and management fees, and no hidden penalties, it may be worth opening the line of credit just to have available as a backup plan.

For landlords, rental properties are a built-in source of capital in your portfolio and could potentially be sold if needed to free up cash, but this potentially comes with a lot of strings attached. Many counties and municipalities have regulations requiring you to pay tenants hefty sums to move out for a sale or requiring new buyers to make these payments, something that can deter potential buyers. And if you haven't lived in the property for two of the last five years, you'll be required to pay capital gains tax on the full amount of property appreciation at your marginal tax rate. Still, if you're truly hard up for funds, selling a property or two may be your best option. Just know what's involved in your particular circumstances.

While going back to work full-time may not be an option when you most need it, that's not to say there's no way to earn money. Make a point of maintaining at least one marketable skill that you could put to use if need be, even if it's in a very part-time capacity, and keep an eye on general trends affecting the industry that your skills fit into. The hope is that you'll never need to put this backup plan into action, but if you do, you'll feel so much better knowing where to begin rather than flailing because you feel lost about how to jump back into the job market or gig economy.

Two final backup sources of capital that aren't ideal to tap but you should still keep in mind are funds in Roth accounts and expected Social Security payments. Remember that contributions to your Roth account may be withdrawn penalty-free at any time, and that Roth conversion contributions may be withdrawn without penalty after the five-year waiting period has elapsed. (Earnings may be withdrawn penalty-free after you're 59½ and the account has been open for five years.) So even if you're planning a two-phase retirement in which you don't touch your tax-advantaged accounts until after 59½, this may be a case for converting at least some funds into a Roth IRA as soon as you're able, to serve as an added emergency fund. In an ideal world, you wouldn't rely on Social Security to fund your retirement, given the status of the program, but in terms of contingency planning, if you're close to an age at which you can claim Social Security benefits and you are running low on funds now, it's an option to spend down some of your other reserves in the near term and then shift to Social Security to pad your standard of living after you reach those years. But explore other options like part-time work first, before you empty out your savings.

Maintain the Right Insurance

While insurance is not a guarantee that you'll never have large, out-of-pocket expenses, carrying the right insurance in early retirement will insulate you financially against some of the worst challenges. We've discussed at length the importance of maintaining excellent health insurance. According to Families USA, two-thirds of medical bankruptcies happen among people with health insurance—and that's a stat that reflects the passage of the Affordable Care Act, when many more people are insured now. It's a critical reminder not just to stay insured but also to keep yourself protected by solid insurance with good coverage levels and a reasonable out-of-pocket maximum that you could theoretically afford to pay every year. If paying a particular plan's out-of-pocket maximum for a few years would devastate your early retirement finances, find another insurance plan with a lower max.

Property insurance is another essential. The form of insurance you get depends on what your living situation is. If you own your home, make sure you are well covered by homeowners insurance for all the normal things, as well as whatever natural disasters are more likely in your area. For example, where we live in California, we are in both wildfire and earthquake risk areas, so we've made sure that we're covered for both. If you do live in California, be aware that deductibles for earthquakes are several times higher than deductibles for normal disasters, by law, and you may have to come up with more than $20,000 in the event an earthquake destroys your home. If you live in an area at risk of flooding, do not skimp on flood insurance. In many areas hit by recent floods, 80% or more of homeowners did not have flood insurance. Flood insurance may be expensive, but it's far cheaper than losing your entire property investment and having to start from scratch. If you're a renter or a full-time RVer, make sure you have solid renters insurance or RV insurance to cover all of your belongings. And in all cases, make sure your property insurance includes some coverage for liability, so that if someone is injured in or around your home and sues you, it doesn't wipe you out financially.

If your early retirement plan involves building up sizeable assets, approaching $1 million or more, it's wise to add umbrella insurance to your policy list. Umbrella insurance is additional liability protection against lawsuits and claims against you, and the data show that high-net-worth people are far more likely to be sued than are those without sizeable assets. You can get protection of $1 million or more for a few hundred dollars a year if you already have liability protection on your property. The best part is that what you're really paying for is the insurance company's legal defense, because they don't want to pay out a single dollar. Umbrella insurance is well worth the cost.

Some types of insurance that you may wish to maintain for a period of time or depending on your circumstances include disability income insurance, term life insurance, and long-term care insurance. You may have some or all of these available to you through your employer, and if you have people depending on your income while you're working, it's a good idea to take advantage of these often low-cost employer-based options, at least while you're working. After you've retired early, you may very well call yourself self-insured, in that you've already saved up whatever money you would need to provide for others and yourself, and you may no longer need these policies, especially disability income and term life insurance. In our case, we bought term life policies in our 20s that are good for 30 years, so we'll continue paying the low cost of them until they expire in our 50s, and then won't renew them. But we do not pay for additional disability income insurance given that we no longer rely on employment income. As to whether long-term care insurance makes sense for you, much depends on where and how you live. Again, Medicare covers very little long-term care in facilities like nursing homes and rehabilitation centers, but it's much more generous with in-home care. If you own your home and it's equipped so that you could stay there if you were in a wheelchair or hospital bed, or it could be retrofitted to accommodate you, then you may be able to skip paying for long-term care insurance and instead opt for in-home care should you ever need it. If, however, you are a long-term renter, full-time traveler, or full-time RVer without a permanent home base that you can modify to fit your needs, then you may opt to buy long-term care insurance so that you know you'll be provided for should you need to receive nursing home care in your later years. The younger you are when you buy long-term care insurance, the lower the premium costs are, but unlike other forms of insurance like term life, the benefit amounts can shift over time, so it pays to shop around and to keep an eye on policy changes each year.

Anticipate Splitting Up or Divorce

It's not a subject that anyone in a couple wants to plan for, but divorce is not a rare phenomenon. Even with divorce rates decreasing among Gen X and Millennial couples compared to Baby Boomers at the same ages, we're still seeing more than a third of all marriages end in divorce. If you've planned your early retirement magic number as a couple, there's a good chance that each of you leaving the marriage with 50% of that number (assuming an equal split, which may or may not apply in your situation) would not let you stay in the work-optional category. So don't shy away from talking about the possibility of divorce. Talking about divorce doesn't make it more likely to happen. Ask yourselves: What would you do financially if you decide to end the marriage? Would it give you both more peace of mind to pad your magic number a bit more, so that you would both still be okay if you had to split up the assets? If you have kids, how would you support them? Could you maintain a very part-time side gig as a general contingency so that you'd have an income stream you could scale up at any time, but with the added benefit of giving you a way to get back into the workforce if you divorced? Though Mark and I did not initially plan our magic number around the idea that we each wanted to be *independently* financially independent, instead of financially interdependent, thanks to good luck with market timing we oversaved and happened to end up with enough that we'd each be okay if we split things 50/50. In hindsight, we wish we had planned to save that much, but either way, it's comforting that, just as we wouldn't want to have to be forced to stay at a job we disliked just for the money, we won't ever feel forced to stay together because of it. It might sound deeply unromantic to think that way, but I think it's the exact opposite. Knowing that we're together 100% by choice and that money plays no part in keeping us together—not even a little bit—is extra romantic and relationship affirming.

Create Your Estate Plan

If you have a partner, children, or anyone else you want to be sure has clear access to your assets after you're gone, then you'll want to be sure to have a strong estate plan in place as soon as possible. Depending on the laws in your state, it may not always be clear that your spouse gets automatic access to your accounts, especially if you have children from a prior marriage or other circumstances that create legal confusion. At a minimum, make sure you have a will and a durable power of attorney in place to make your wishes clear, and consider adding an advanced health care directive to simplify health care decision-making on your behalf. You can create all of these documents yourself using reputable and affordable online services like Nolo or LegalZoom. If you wish to engage an estate attorney, keep an eye out for unnecessary add-ons that they may try to push. Financial experts say you do not need a revocable living trust in most circumstances, and an estate attorney who insists that you do is just trying to pad your bill. Find another attorney to work with. Estate planning is also important if leaving behind a charitable legacy is important to you, even if you do not have heirs. Write your will to specify how you'd like your assets divided when you pass on, and update the beneficiaries on all of your financial and insurance accounts to reflect whom you'd like to receive the funds.

Learn the Rules to Reduce Health Care Costs When Necessary

With health care costs rising faster than inflation and ongoing political debates about health care raging, there's a lot of uncertainty out there around health insurance, but if you learn the rules of the current system, you'll always be able to minimize your health care costs if you are in a bind financially. So long as the Affordable Care Act stays in effect, you may be able to reverse-engineer your income to stay within particular confines so that you become eligible for great health care at the lowest price. The ACA doesn't cap how much premiums can go up each year in general, but it does dictate the percentage of your income that you can spend on insurance premiums, so therefore, the lower your income, the lower your out-of-pocket health care costs. If you have the flexibility to choose how many shares of index funds you sell, for example, then you'll always have a contingency plan to insulate yourself against rising health care costs during a bad sequence of returns years or other times of hardship.

The ideal sweet spot if you're optimizing your income for health care is to get your modified adjusted gross income (MAGI—all of your taxable income minus any new contributions to IRA or non-Roth retirement accounts) to fall just above the Medicaid-eligibility threshold for your state and family size, which is 138% of the federal poverty level (FPL) in most states. In 2018, the federal poverty level was $12,140 for individuals, $16,460 for a couple or family of two, $25,100 for a family of four, up to $42,380 for a family of eight, and it is generally adjusted upward each year. (Levels are higher in Alaska and Hawaii.) So, for example, for a family of four, keeping your MAGI as close to $34,638 (138% of FPL at 2018 levels) without going under it will keep you out of Medicaid (or no coverage, in a state that hasn't expanded Medicaid), and make you eligible for an enhanced ACA exchange plan at an extremely low cost. The most subsidized plans, sometimes called Enhanced Silver, cover up to 94% of expenses, have premiums of only a few dollars a month, and give you completely normal health insurance with a private insurer.

While that income level may sound low, depending on your circumstances, remember that not all money you have to spend in early retirement will count in MAGI because not all of it is new income. Dividends from your investments count as income, as does rental income after you subtract expenses, along with any actual work you do. But if you sell shares of stocks or bonds, only the gains—the difference between what you paid and what the shares are now worth—are considered income. Depending how much your portfolio has grown, your gains may not make up a large portion of your portfolio, and therefore you may be able to withdraw a sizeable amount without triggering much increase in your taxable income and MAGI. In addition, distributions from Roth accounts do not count as income for tax and health purposes, though new Roth conversions do. If you can get your income into this range, you're also likely to owe very little income tax. Each December, before the tax year and health-care open enrollment ends, total up everything you've earned—both earned and unearned income—and decide whether you have additional room under your health care and tax threshold targets to sell additional shares, or to do Roth conversions, and proceed accordingly.

Stay Current on Financial Developments

After you've saved up your work-optional portfolio, and you've done your math on how much you can safely spend each year, don't check out. Stay current on the latest in early retirement analysis, investment performance, and emerging strategies for maximizing your money. All of the strategies included in this book will give you the highest reasonable likelihood of success. But innovators will surely come along who may find ways that you can spend slightly more and increase your standard of living while still stretching your portfolio for your full life span. And the best investment options may shift over time. When that happens, you want to know about it.

BULLETPROOF PLANNING CHECKLIST

- ☐ Determine your asset allocation for both long-term growth and risk management.
- ☐ Decide which withdrawal strategy you'll use.
- ☐ Create your bare-bones budget and determine how you'll cut expenses if you need to.

- [ ] Determine what your sources of backup capital will be.
- [ ] Make sure you have adequate insurance for your circumstances.
- [ ] Create your estate plan.
- [ ] If you have a partner, discuss how you'll handle divorce or splitting up.
- [ ] Determine how you could optimize your income to reduce health care costs, if needed.
- [ ] Stay current on financial analysis impacting retirement account, withdrawal strategy, etc.

PART III

THRIVING IN YOUR WORK-OPTIONAL LIFE

Fast-forward to the moment when you can say you've done it. You've achieved your version of early retirement, whatever that looks like to you, and you're ready to embark on your new work-optional life. Let's talk about the practical steps to take to ensure that this new life you're living is everything you dreamed it would be.

CHAPTER 10

Make the Big Leap

Life is traveling to the edge of knowledge, then a leap taken.
—D. H. LAWRENCE

December 29, 2017, was the first day of my new life chapter, when I woke up with nowhere to be, no conference calls on the calendar, and no immediate to-do list. It took some time before I truly felt "retired," because it takes time to adapt to any transition, but also because that word still feels like something that only people in their 60s or 70s do, regardless of how long we'd been planning for and I'd been writing about early retirement. I remember the exact day, though, when it clicked that I didn't have to work, when I thought, *I actually feel retired now.* Mark and I were on mountain bikes, racing down the narrow road through Taroko Gorge in Taiwan, a spectacular white marble canyon that ought to be better known in the West than it is, doing our best not to get hit by tour buses while taking it all in. It was a Monday, we had no idea what time it was back home, we had no cell service or Wi-Fi, and for the first time in years, neither of us felt any impulse to check our phones. We were fully present and in no rush to be anywhere else. *This is what it's all about*, I thought.

And while that was the day things clicked for me, I've since realized that I don't have to be in the middle of some epic bucket list adventure to feel retired. I don't have to be in a stone house in the south of France, in a gorge in Taiwan, or atop a 14,000-foot peak in the High Sierra. I feel retired when I get eight hours of sleep, which is almost every day now. I feel retired when I leave the house without my phone or go hours without checking it. I even feel retired when I do things that look a lot like work, because I know it's work I'm choosing to do. (Though I feel even more retired still when I drop whatever work I was planning to do that day to ski or hang out with friends instead.)

That's because I realized a few months into our work-optional life that retirement itself isn't about never contributing to society again. It isn't even about whether you work or not. It's about having the freedom to control your own time and to decide for yourself how to spend your focus and attention. And the feeling of that freedom goes way beyond all my expectations.

So let's project forward to this moment for you. You've now spent some time saving, you've changed your view on money and life, and you've made your big transition. Congrats! This is really happening! So now what? Let's talk about making the leap from a life dictated by the rules of work to a life you live on your terms and getting to a place mentally where you feel the freedom that comes with knowing you're in charge of your own life, beginning with the logistical steps that will set you up to rock your transition.

Preparing to Leave Work

Whether you're leaving a career, transitioning to part-time, or taking a career intermission, you want to be thoughtful about when and how you make your leap, as well as how you tell people. The first question is timing. Are there factors you want to time your exit around, like a year-end bonus or a 401(k) match? Mark and I had always planned to leave our careers on the same day, but as it happened, I had to work a few days longer to get my company's 401(k) match. While it was a tiny bummer that he got to wake up with nowhere to be a few days before I did, it was a no-brainer to work a few more days in exchange for a several-thousand-dollar company match, while still retiring at essentially the same time. Make sure you're factoring in financial aspects like that before you plan your exit date, particularly if you have reason to believe that you might not receive a bonus if the company knows you're leaving. Even if you're transitioning to part-time work with the same company, part-time positions often have fewer benefits, and so it's essential to think through everything you might lose when you're no longer full-time and account for that in your timing. Additionally, you may have factors that are more personal or carry meaning to you in terms of career achievements. Perhaps you want to see the completion of a project you've invested yourself in for a long time, or you want to get someone you mentor promoted. If you have kids, you may wish to time your exit to coincide with the end of a school year so that you maximize your summer time with them. Or you may decide to retire in the spring so that there are plenty of opportunities to get outside in your initial retired weeks and months, and you don't feel cooped up indoors, factors that may ease your transition. Your last work day may be timed around a range of factors, both personal and financial, so ask yourself what timing would make your exit feel best in your circumstances.

If you're in a couple, talk well in advance of your exits. In addition to the added tension staggered retirements may bring, if you leave work at very different times, one of you may miss out on having the support and camaraderie of someone going through the same big life transition you're experiencing. Make sure you both consider timing thoroughly before announcing your plans at work.

In the last year or so before you give notice, keep your ears open for talk of buyouts or early retirement offers. Often you must have been with an employer for an extended period to take advantage of such packages, but not always. And even if you haven't hit your magic number, the addition of a lump sum from a buyout package might be enough to push you over your goal.

Also, in that last year of full-time work, assuming you have employer-provided health insurance, it's an ideal time to use as much health care as you might possibly need. Think of it like preventive maintenance. You want to get every bodily system checked and get the all-clear on your health while you still have what's probably more generous health insurance than you're likely to have if you buy an exchange plan. If there are any little medical mysteries in your life that you've put off thinking about, the last year of traditional employment is a good time to play health care detective and get the answers you need. Mark and I each saw multiple specialists and got some recommended tests and vaccines a little early in our last year of work, knowing our costs to get the same care the next year would be higher. This may also be the last time you have dental or vision coverage, so use those benefits, too. I got several fillings replaced just before leaving, knowing there'd never be a cheaper time to do it, and Mark and I each got the most thorough eye exams of our lives.

Finally, if you're traditionally employed, you need to decide how much notice to give your employer and what to tell them you're going to be doing. Several people we know, when giving their employers the news, did not tell them that they were retiring early, saying instead that they were resigning to focus on other priorities. While I understand their reasoning, I think this is a mistake. Leaving that way implies that you're unhappy, which leaves a bad impression behind when you go. But leaving to retire early and move on to the next chapter of your life feels more celebratory and like it has less to do with your employer or your dissatisfaction. This allows you to leave on a positive note, which may result in the door remaining open if you ever change your mind and decide you'd like to go back. Either way, how much notice you give will be dependent on how senior your role is, but I don't recommend giving too much notice. Three months should be your upper limit. Beyond that, people tend to feel like lame ducks at work and don't enjoy the feeling of having to continue to show up while feeling irrelevant. But given that you are retiring and don't have another opportunity you're rushing off to, it's respectful to give more than two weeks' notice. A good balance is often between four and eight weeks.

If you are hoping to stop working full-time but continue to work with the same company in a part-time or consulting capacity, you may wish to give a bit more notice and allow time for some negotiation about what your new arrangement could look like. Go in prepared to make a strong case about why the company should agree to your hoped-for schedule, just as you would prepare to ask for a raise or promotion, and have a backup plan in the event they say no. Asking for a part-time schedule may also force you to tip your hand about your long-term intentions, and in that case, be cautious and don't share your plans until you've saved all you need to save. Of course, if it's typical in your workplace for people to work reduced schedules, then asking for one may be more a formality than anything and arranging it may be no big deal.

If you're planning a career intermission and hope to leave open the possibility of going back to the same employer, be extra positive throughout the process of giving notice and wrapping up your final weeks. Do excellent-quality work, be a team player, ask where you can be most helpful before you leave, and offer to share your knowledge with those who would benefit from it. You may even find that your employer is so eager to keep you that they'll arrange an official sabbatical for you—usually unpaid leave while remaining on the company books—with an understanding that you can come back to a similar position in six months or a year. In that case, it's worth inquiring about whether you can stay on the company health insurance plan at a rate cheaper than COBRA, continue vesting stock, or in other ways stay connected to the job.

If you work for yourself, you'll have a range of timing choices to make as well, beginning with when to tell your clients, customers, and employees. Depending on how reliant they are on you, you may wish to give them several months or even years of notice, or you may only need to give them a few weeks. If you're scaling back your involvement in a business that will continue operating without you, you'll want time to find someone to step into your role. And if you're hoping to sell your business, you'll want to keep your ears open for leads for perhaps years in advance of your departure. You know the particulars of your business, so plan these various steps into your timeline.

Whichever model of retirement you're pursuing, if someone offers to throw you a goodbye party, take them up on it. Research shows that those who celebrate this big life moment gain enormous benefits from doing so, most notably being able to look back and affirm that you were a valued part of your work community. Those who don't celebrate or feel like no one noticed when they left are more likely to carry around resentment later on.[1] While there's no helping the fact that you will become less relevant as soon as you give notice, harness the excitement people feel for you and make this a *moment*. If your company isn't a very party-oriented place, then throw your own happy hour and invite your team or your work friends.

Here's a checklist of things to do in your final months at work:

- ☐ Choose your timing on when to give notice or to inform your clients and employees.
- ☐ Choose your last day.
- ☐ Plan how you'll send yourself off—retirement party, happy hour, farewell lunch, etc.

☐ Decide which work contacts you may wish to keep in touch with and reach out.

☐ Get as much preventive health care as possible, and take care of anything you've been putting off.

☐ Get any dental or vision care you need.

☐ Decide what health insurance you'll switch to.

☐ Consider adding funding to your donor-advised fund, if that's part of your plan.

☐ Lock down your withdrawal strategy.

☐ Top up your cash accounts.

☐ Consider applying for a home equity line of credit, if that is one of your contingency plans.

☐ Take care of any other costly expenses like vet care or home maintenance while you still have a regular paycheck.

☐ For semiretirees transitioning to self-employment, lay the groundwork for new business ventures so that you can hit the ground running.

☐ Book your first big trip, if you're focused on travel.

☐ Plan how you'll celebrate!

Pulling the Ripcord

Mark and I flew back to DC, where our former employers are based, for our last full week of work, and celebrated our departures with our closest colleagues. And then, just like that, our careers were over. We'd been planning for that moment for years, and yet when it came, it still felt surprisingly enormous. But we'd decided months earlier that we didn't want to finish our last days and then hop on a plane and have it feel like coming home from a normal business trip. So we made a few stops first. The night of our last day at work, we drove down to rural Virginia, where Mark's college roommate has a small organic winery, stopping for a celebratory dinner at Cracker Barrel. It could not have been less extravagant, but it didn't matter. What mattered is we didn't have to check our email constantly that night, that weekend, or the next week—or ever. Conference call hold music would no longer play a major role in our lives. We wouldn't get stressed out about falling behind in our work due to having a fun weekend to ourselves. We were done! And sitting on the rocking chairs in front of the restaurant felt exactly right. We knew we weren't going to have the sit-in-a-rocking-chair variety of retirement, but it marked the beginning of the transition for us. From there, we enjoyed a mellow weekend with friends, and then flew to New Orleans for a few days. By the time we arrived home five days later, work felt far away, which was just as we'd intended. I still had to work those last two days remotely for the 401(k) match, but those days barely registered in my mind. I already felt different.

So back to you. Your last day of full-time employment has arrived, and now it's time to begin your next adventure. Right away after leaving traditional employment—after you've celebrated, of course—make sure to take care of these logistics:

- ☐ Ensure you have no gap in health coverage by either signing up for an ACA plan right away or getting on your former employer's COBRA plan. Leaving your job gives you a special enrollment period to sign up for new coverage, but do it ASAP. It's also possible, if you know your work separation date, to sign up for new coverage before you actually leave your job, so do this as soon as you can.
- ☐ If you had a phone or computer through work, you may need to replace it. Look for low-cost service with no contract, especially Wi-Fi-first cell plans that cost a fraction of what traditional plans charge.

☐ Reconsider all of your home tech needs. For example, if you worked from home, you may have a landline you no longer need or faster internet than you require. Scale back as appropriate.

☐ Replace any additional insurance that you got through work that you still need, like term life insurance.

☐ Take first monthly or quarterly withdrawal from your brokerage account, if using a drawdown investment strategy, paying attention to what tax year the capital gains will fall into and how that affects your income tax.

☐ Set up your cash flow systems to replicate a paycheck, if you need that to stay on track. For example, you may open a new checking account that serves as your holding account when you sell shares or receive rent payments, and then automatically transfer to your regular checking account your monthly amount to spend so it still feels like receiving paychecks. You might also opt to keep a separate checking account as a parking lot for large expenses you know are coming, like property tax, quarterly income taxes, and car insurance.

☐ Continue tracking your spending to stay on course.

These tasks don't need to happen immediately, but within the first few months of leaving employment, take care of the following:

☐ Decide whether to roll over your 401(k) or another employer-based plan to an IRA. If your employer plan has low fees and expense ratios, and you like the fund options, there's no need to move your funds, but if you can get lower fees or better fund choices elsewhere, then do a direct rollover to IRA to avoid paying high fees for too long. Make sure to arrange the rollover to go directly from your old plan to your new brokerage, or you'll be hit with a mandatory income tax withholding and some extra hoops to jump through. Note that once you leave your employer's 401(k), you cannot go back, so consider your options carefully before making the switch. Also note that if part of your 401(k) or 403(b) was funded by pretax dollars and part by after-tax dollars, you may wish to roll the pretax portion over to a traditional IRA and the after-tax portion over to a Roth IRA.

☐ Begin Roth conversions if you wish to use that strategy. You have until the end of the calendar year to make conversions, but many brokerages will require you to open the new account several months sooner even if you don't convert all the funds you wish to convert for the year in that transaction.

☐ Assess whether your new spending matches what you anticipated or is higher or lower. If it's lower, great! Enjoy the wiggle room in your budget. If it's higher, look for mindless spending that has snuck in, or begin strategizing ways to earn a little extra to cover the overage.

☐ Assess whether you'll likely owe federal and/or state income tax on your early retirement income, and therefore need to pay estimated quarterly taxes. The first quarter payment is due on Tax Day in April, and there is a penalty if you underpay. Consult the resources in the Additional Resources section of this book for information on federal estimated quarterly taxes, and your state tax authority if applicable.

The Emotional Side of the Transition

Beyond the logistical to-do list, you're now in the midst of a huge life transition, so it's important to take care of your full self. Give yourself a detox period to release all that work stress you've been carrying around for years. Depending on whether you're now fully work-optional or just scaling back or taking a break from work, you'll calibrate your detox period accordingly, but make time to catch up on sleep and to have plenty of unscheduled time to do nothing but relax. Many early retirees report needing at least six months to a year to feel caught up on sleep and to establish a new set of routines, so give this process lots of time. This might also be a good time to make a symbolic gesture to yourself to signal the closing of one life chapter and the opening of another. After I gave notice, I swapped out the discreet stud I had in my nose for a much more visible hoop and dyed my hair purple, both things I never could have done while climbing the career ladder. Your gesture need not be visible to anyone but you. Maybe it's donating all your suits and work clothes to Dress for Success or Goodwill. Perhaps it's getting rid of the vehicle you no longer need. Maybe it's taking a few minutes to jump on the bed to signal to yourself that you're now allowed to relive the best parts of childhood. If there's something that pops out at you as the right thing to do to mark the transition, that's your answer.

The sociologist Robert S. Weiss conducted one of the most extensive surveys ever among people going through the retirement transition, which he documented in his book *The Experience of Retirement*. Much of this research is directly relevant to early retirees because it has nothing to do with age. For example, Weiss found that there are very real losses that come from retirement, most notably a loss of community, life structure, and personal identity. But he also found that the gains far outweigh the losses for most people. The biggest gain is the freedom from work stress and work obligations and newfound freedom in how to spend time. In addition, those who had been subject to high work stress believed that it made them bad parents and spouses, and being free of that stress made them more present and supportive in their relationships.

Despite the massive excitement you'll likely feel, any form of retirement can still be inherently stressful because it's such a big life event. So it's not unusual to feel some sadness or even to mourn the loss of your old career or career identity, though these feelings need not detract from the happy ones. Just allow space for both. And whenever you feel like celebrating, celebrate! You've just done an amazing thing, and the feeling of euphoric disbelief may last a while. Enjoy it.

The biggest question you'll face in the short term is whether you thrive in an unstructured time environment or need some structure. This may very well be the first extended time in your life when no one else has told you where you need to be and when. For some people, the lack of structure will be a beautiful thing, giving you time to get to know yourself in a totally new way. However, for others, the lack of structure will make it feel like you never get anything done, and the days just slip by. Weiss's research also found that, beyond structure, many retirees find that they miss the discipline that work forces on them. As he puts it, "The freedom to do anything includes the freedom to remain engaged as well as the freedom to do nothing." Suddenly, it's easy to stay in bed or on the couch all day rather than check things off your list. This combination of not having anywhere to be and not having anyone check up on whether you're getting things done may cause you to feel like you're drifting aimlessly. If you notice that happening, it's simply a signal that you need to either develop internal discipline you never required before or create systems for yourself just like you did with your automated investing.

There's no right or wrong answer, so notice what feels true for you. Go back to the exercises we did in part I to remind yourself what an ideal day looks like. Are you naturally finding yourself doing the things that ideal day would entail, or do you need a nudge to get you off the couch? There's nothing wrong with needing nudges or structures, and if you find that you do need some, consider scheduling set activities or blocking out days for certain tasks. Or structure might come from giving yourself incentives: If you finish this task, then you get to have ice cream after dinner, for example. Experiment with what type of structure or incentives feel helpful without limiting your ability to do what you feel drawn to do each day.

If you have a partner, this detox period can also be a wonderful time to refocus on your relationship, especially given how damaging work demands can be to partnerships. Make time for each other and communicate a lot during this period, especially what you're each feeling as you decompress from work and adjust to your new life rhythms. One study found that couples retiring tend to experience an increase in conflict during the first year or two after retirement, whether they retire together or in a more staggered way. But this conflict lowers over time, eventually settling into a level lower than it was during your working years.[2] Anticipating and acknowledging that the life transition will come with both positive and negative feelings for both of you will make your temporary conflict easier to deal with. You may find that you have new needs or different preferences now. One of you may crave structure after it's gone, and the other may thrive without it. Or you may find that one of you needs more time alone or out of the house than the other does. Stay in sync about what you each need as you work through the transition and take joy in establishing new joint routines, making sure that some of those new routines involve communicating more. Set aside couple time such as weekly date nights or phone-free evenings to ensure that you aren't just in the same place, but you're also talking regularly.

If you have kids, you may wonder how to instill in them a strong work ethic if you're no longer going to work all day, every day. It's a mistake to assume that just going to work every day will teach kids to work hard in life. A parent who comes home every day complaining about work will instill exactly the wrong beliefs in a child, that work is bad and something not to invest yourself in. So if you know you've been a complainer, removing the complaint itself will be a positive on its own. But using your new free time to model to your kids how to be active in your community or how to invest yourself in a project of your own making and do your best work, all the while encouraging and supporting them in school, will help them have a strong model to emulate, even if you're not following the traditional career path any longer.

Some other to-do list items you might consider tackling during this detox period include:

- ☐ Stop setting an alarm clock.
- ☐ Move your phone and devices out of the bedroom entirely, to help break bad tech habits.
- ☐ If you used to work from home, repaint and rearrange your office space to create new associations with that part of your home.
- ☐ Sell or donate unneeded work clothes.
- ☐ Set date nights with your partner, even if it's just to go for a walk, to share how you're each feeling in the transition.
- ☐ Plan a trip or an adventure for after you catch up on sleep.
- ☐ Make a personal gesture to signal the start of your new life chapter.

You may find yourself tempted to do everything on your to-do list right away, but be careful not to take on too much too quickly. Focus on rest and relaxation for the first few months, and then add in new tasks or commitments one at a time. Even with plenty of newfound free time, it's easy to feel busy again, so take it slow in saying yes to new things.

If you're taking a career intermission, a useful strategy might be to think of your time in blocks. Consider giving yourself two weeks to do nothing but catch up on sleep and relax. Then take two weeks to knock out projects around the house or other lingering to-do list tasks. Then get on with your planned adventures, leaving some breaks in between trips or busy travel days for self-care and rest. You want to arrive back at work at the end of your time off feeling well rested and ready to jump back in, not exhausted and overwhelmed, so prioritize lots of chillout time just as you would if you were retiring permanently.

These initial weeks and months of your work-optional life will be a time of learning a lot about yourself. We spend virtually all of our lives with our time scheduled for us, either in school or at work, or perhaps in providing care to children or other loved ones, and having the gift of abundant free time will likely reveal a whole new side of yourself that you may not know very well. And you now have time to get to know this person.

CHAPTER 11

Make Your Well-Being a Top Priority

A healthy attitude is contagious, but don't wait to catch it from others. Be a carrier.

—TOM STOPPARD

In our final years of work, Mark and I both saw our health deteriorate from job stress. I got frequent migraines and lived with near-constant back pain. His autoimmune disease flared up more often, disrupting what kind of activities he could do and requiring expensive medication. We knew that leaving our careers would improve our health, but we let ourselves fall into some magical thinking that our health would improve instantly with no effort on our part, merely because we'd no longer have job stress weighing on us. And while subtracting that stress from our lives did make us both feel better, we quickly understood that we needed to be active participants in keeping ourselves healthy in early retirement and later in traditional retirement. The truth is, it's incredibly easy to be lazy when you have nowhere to be (especially if you have a big, comfy couch like we do, and years of Netflix to catch up on). Early retirement itself will not magically make healthy choices for you, reverse your bad habits, or get you off the couch. You still have to make the conscious choice and effort to live the life you dream of. The best thing you can do to make sure that happens is to prioritize your physical, mental, and emotional well-being.

Healthy Up Your Lifestyle

It's absolutely worthwhile to prioritize your physical well-being now that you have more time and have removed a lot of the work stress so many of us suffer from. (It's even better if you can focus on your health beginning today, and not wait until you get to your work-optional life.) There's the other side of health, too—what you might think of as your spiritual or metaphysical well-being. This could have religious meaning to you, or it could just mean feeling closely connected to others and in tune with the world around you. Both types of well-being are important for your long-term health.

Now that you have the incredible luxury of more time, the first area to focus on will likely be getting more exercise. Research shows that most Americans are more sedentary than doctors recommend we should be, and this is all the more true for workers with desk jobs. Where you begin will have everything to do with where you're starting. If you're generally athletic but have let yourself get out of shape while working, you'll have a different plan of attack than someone who's never been active before. Consult your doctor or physical therapist if you're challenged in your mobility or have a medical issue like diabetes or high blood pressure to understand what's safe for you. Otherwise, if you have good mobility, start wherever on the checklist is appropriate for your current fitness level, consulting a physician first if you have any concerns about your underlying health:

- ☐ Get up and move around for at least 30 minutes every day.
- ☐ Aim for 10,000 steps per day, which you can track on most smartphones without a separate fitness tracker.
- ☐ Do as many tasks and chores around the house as possible yourself rather than outsourcing them to keep you active and strong.

☐ Explore different types of activity, from walking and running, to swimming and cycling, dancing and kickboxing, or more adventurous pursuits like backpacking and rock-climbing—many of these can be done for free or for little cost through community colleges, churches, and community centers.

☐ Make a fitness plan for yourself that includes a mixture of cardio (heart-pumping) exercise and load-bearing exercise (lifting weights, hiking with a backpack, functional strength training) to keep your bones and muscles strong as you get older.

☐ Commit to a regular course of classes if you enjoy the group exercise setting.

☐ Consider hiring a personal trainer for a limited period to give you a customized exercise plan appropriate to your current abilities and interests.

☐ Enroll in a recreational sports league in your community, like adult soccer or volleyball, to force yourself to stay active with a side of social interaction.

☐ Sign up for a race or other fitness event to keep you accountable to a training schedule.

☐ Plan for a more epic adventure, like climbing a mountain or cycling across your state, and then train to do it.

☐ Continue exploring new forms of fitness and exercise to keep it interesting.

☐ Sign up for events regularly if they keep you motivated to stay active, enroll in new group exercise classes, or buy a personal training package every few months. Having a date on the calendar or having money sunk into your fitness will encourage you to stay accountable and active.

Our society makes it so cheap and convenient to eat unhealthily these days, but now that you have the gift of more time, you can focus on preparing more of your own meals and taking care to make them healthy. Ignore fad diets, which are generally shown to be expensive and ineffective, and focus on eating as much fresh, unprocessed food as possible, without adding a lot of sugar, salt, or fat. If you've never paid attention to what you eat before, it's a great investment to take a community college course in nutrition or consult with a nutritionist (this may be partially covered by your health insurance), but research shows that cooking more meals from scratch improves health while also strengthening family bonds, so it's a win-win. Plus, cooking can be a ton of fun! Here are some ways you can healthy up your eating habits after you have more time on your hands:

- Shop the perimeter of your grocery store, and avoid the freezer and pantry sections.
- Set a goal of cooking one meal from scratch every day.
- Swap out quick foods like sugar-rich instant oatmeal for healthier but slower (and cheaper!) rolled oats or steel cut oats that you cook.
- Take a cooking class to learn new skills.
- Try one new recipe a week to expand your repertoire.
- Learn to re-create your favorite restaurant dishes at home, going easy on the sugar, salt, and fat, and increasing the vegetable content.
- Buy a CSA share or farm box so you always have fresh fruit and vegetables in the house.
- Buy one vegetable you've never tried before each month and experiment with cooking it different ways.
- Start a garden, and grow all your favorite veggies.

- Get to know the vendors at your local farmers market—they may give you a deal if they consider you a friend.
- Ask farmers at the market if they would trade work for produce, such as a box of organic veggies if you staff the booth for them each week.

While exercise and diet are hugely important components of maintaining and improving your physical health so you can get as much enjoyment as possible out of your new life, it's still important to get regular medical care. Regardless of which health insurance you have, and even if it's a high-deductible plan, the Affordable Care Act dictates that your insurance must completely cover one preventive care doctor visit each year. Use it! Get your annual physical every year, and while you're there, get a flu shot and have all the basic bloodwork done to check for high cholesterol, hormonal changes, and metabolic conditions like diabetes or liver disease. Those services are guaranteed to you for free by law, and too many people—even people with insurance—are not taking advantage of them. Stay on top of your preventive care so that if something does pop up, you'll know about it earlier, when it's more treatable and perhaps less expensive to treat. By law, your plan must also provide you with mental health services, so make use of them if you need them. Even early retired people can get depressed or feel anxious and decide that counseling would be beneficial. Taking the best care of yourself means seeking out mental health care just as you would seek out care you need to keep yourself well physically.

If you have had a number of healthy years in a row, don't assume that you'll be healthy forever and cheap out on your health insurance or fail to budget for your plan's out-of-pocket maximum. You always want to know that you can afford to get the care you need so that you never let cost concerns stand in the way of getting treatment when you're sick. We learned this the hard way only a few months into retirement. I came down with a severe stomach bug, and it was clear I needed to go to the hospital, but I waited hours longer than I should have because I knew we hadn't met our fairly high deductible and would be on the hook for the entire cost of the emergency room trip. We learned an important lesson from that: In our case, lower deductibles are better, because they remove the psychological barrier to seeking care, and we adjusted accordingly when we renewed our insurance, paying a little more each month to bring that deductible down.

The Importance of Social Connections to Your Well-Being

When we think about health, we tend to think about our bodies only. But here's a fact that may surprise you: The people who live the longest and have the highest number of healthy years are those with the closest social connections.[1] It turns out that cultivating strong social circles is a hugely important component in protecting your physical health. While early retirement gives you more free time to spend with people, you also lose the community you had at work. The social circles you cultivated while saving for early retirement may not be at a similar place in the journey, or they may be primarily online friends. An added challenge is that if you retire early but none of your friends do, you might unexpectedly find that no one is available to hang out when you want to. So make up your mind now that you're not going to be blindsided by this fact and that you're going to find ways to become a part of new communities as well that carry meaning for you. Without that effort, you may find that early retirement is surprisingly isolating, which is not only bad for your health but also boring. Marriage and close family ties are important, but they do not cover all of your social needs. If you're living life and getting out of the house, chances are good that you'll meet plenty of new people organically, and then the trick is really just in taking the step of asking them to get together again or asking to join their group.

One of Mark's and my favorite things about living in a ski region like Lake Tahoe is that most people work untraditional schedules here. Let's face it: You're not moving to Tahoe to bolster your career unless that career is in ski racing. People move to places like this for the lifestyle and then find ways to hustle enough so that they can make it work to stay, which is like what we've done, except in reverse. When we were working, we were the weird ones who could only ski on the weekends instead of going out when the crowds were smaller on the weekdays, and it tore at us every time friends invited us to go out for a hike or mountain bike ride in the middle of a work-day and we had to say no. But we knew that the short-term pain of saying no was a worthwhile trade-off for the long-term benefit we'd receive from living here, which is that there are more people gener-ally whose schedules match those of early retirees. And as an added benefit, the culture is both outdoorsy and frugal, so there's always someone up for going out for a paddle or a hike and packing a lunch to enjoy while you're out there. Ski towns tend to be expensive places to live, and that's certainly true here, but we find that we spend very little on recreation and social time, which makes up for a lot of that cost. And even if the mountains or small towns don't speak to you as where you'd like to be for the long term, it's worth considering if the place you see yourself has people you have something in common with who will be around to hang out during your free time, when everyone else is at work. College towns and cities with big creative communities are especially great for that, along with obvious places like beach communities. Whether you crave a life in the city, the suburbs, or in a more natural rural area, considering how the culture of the place you call home will impact your health and social interactions before you retire early will pay off big time.

But either way, whether there are plenty of people around midday or not, start by looking around at the places where you're spending your newfound time. Are there people you meet at the gym who seem interesting or whom you've bumped into on the same trails multiple times? Even if someone doesn't look familiar to you, maybe strike up a conversation with the person buying paintbrushes next to you at the art supply store or browsing the historical novel selection at the library—you have time to chat now, and don't need to rush off to the next thing. You may find that you meet kindred spirits with whom you have a shared interest and perhaps a shared schedule.

If the organic, spontaneous approach isn't your thing, consider what new clubs you can join as a way to meet new people and join new communities. Local college alumni groups are an easy place for college grads to start, and there are Meetup groups out there for virtually every possible interest. It can feel a little bit like trying to date again, but if you meet someone interesting, ask them out for a friend date. See if they'd be up for a coffee or beer, or if they'd like to come to your next backyard get-together and figure out if they're friend material. Oftentimes the hardest part of making friends is just finding the courage to ask, but it helps to remind yourself that nearly everyone wishes they had more of this courage. You're most likely doing others a favor if you make the overture, and many will be grateful you did, in addition to being new friends.

Many parents naturally find that having kids limits their social circle to parents of other kids the same age as theirs, but shifting into a work-optional life is a great time to create new friendships among people with whom you share more interests in common beyond your kids.

And finally, don't let yourself feel limited by age. If you're retiring very young, that shouldn't stop you from befriending older retirees, and you might even be surprised what you can learn from their experience with traditional retirement. Regardless of when we retire, we face many of the same challenges with loss of identity and creating a new sense of structure and meaning in life. And everyone should make a point of befriending some people younger than you. Because early retirement takes you out of the workplace, where many of us learn about new trends and technologies, we lose much of the connection to technological shifts as well as other aspects of the current culture. Maintaining friendships with people younger than you helps keep you connected so you won't ever run the risk of feeling old too soon. (And while you're at it, stay up on basic advances in technology. You don't have to buy every new gadget or get on every new social network, but stay generally grounded in what's happening.)

Of course, in addition to making friends, early retirement is a great time to prioritize family as you may not have been able to before. If you have kids, plan some big adventures you can go on together to form lifelong memories, even if they're big adventures in the backyard or city park. If you have far-flung siblings, use your newly flexible schedule to visit them more often. Say yes to the gatherings and reunions you've been too busy for while working. Spend as much time as you can with aging parents if they're still around and help them check off things that are left on their bucket lists. Assisting others in reaching their goals—or even just being there when they do it—can be as rewarding as achieving the goals you set out for yourself.

Think Big About Your Mental and Spiritual Well-Being

For years, when people asked me what I'd actually do after we retired early, I'd answer in all sincerity, "I'll figure out what I want to do when I grow up." I really meant that. Before retiring early, I'd never met the version of me who wasn't feeling the stress of work or school, or the version of me who could envision taking on a personal project that would take more time than a weekend or my few weeks of vacation each year. I'd never met the version of me who could follow my passions without worrying about how well that paid, the version who had nearly infinite possibilities in front of me. I'd never even met the version of me who knew what it felt like to get enough sleep. But now, I have the incredible privilege of getting to know that person, and by listening to the needs of this newly discovered version of me, I'm able to live a life that's much more focused on my physical, mental, and emotional well-being.

Fundamentally, to live a life of optimal well-being, you need to feel personally enriched from continual learning, you need to feel challenged by ongoing growth, and you need validation that tells you you're valued by your community. Or, to put it another way, as shallow as the "What do you do?" question may feel, think about how you want to be able to answer that in your new life in a way that sounds interesting, if not to anyone else, at least to yourself. That may require going against what society tells us we're supposed to do. Research tells us that society most respects those retirees who appear to have a "strenuous" retirement, meaning they appear just as busy and active as people still working full-time.[2] That shouldn't be your driving motivation. Don't strive to look busy. Strive to live a life that you find interesting and that makes you feel connected to communities who value you, regardless of whether you feel social pressure to make your retirement appear a certain way. According to Weiss's research, the ideal scenario is when you spend your time in ways that are both intellectually and emotionally rewarding, reduce vulnerability to social isolation, sustain feelings of worth, and are minimally demanding and stressful. So you should be able to check off all of the following boxes with your new activities:

☐ Continually learn new things.
☐ Receive emotional rewards.
☐ Engage in activities that are social.
☐ Get positive feedback and feel valued.

Go back to part I and the ways you said you wanted to spend your time in your work-optional life, and figure out which boxes you can check off based on what you've already planned to do. For any boxes you didn't check off, consider employing some of the strategies below to give you a well-rounded life that fuels your well-being—and accept that things could change along the way. For example, something that once was a relaxing foil to your high-stress work life, which you imagined would fill hours and hours of your new life, may feel insufferably boring after you aren't so tightly wound anymore. If that happens and you find that you're now missing one of the boxes above, revisit this list.

- **Indulge your curiosity and prioritize lifelong learning:** Humans are naturally curious creatures, and early retirement provides the ultimate opportunity to learn about all the things you've always wanted to know. So indulge that interest! Sign up for community college classes, take online language courses, watch YouTube videos to learn new DIY skills you can use around the house (bonus: save money vs. hiring contractors), try those new types of fitness activities, and begin thinking of yourself as a student of life. Doing so will give you an endless font of intellectual rewards.
- **Replicate what you were best at in your work:** In chapter 8, we talked about reflecting on what you're best at in your job as a way to fend off impatience and keep yourself focused on the positives at work. If you get to early retirement and

realize that you miss doing what you were best at, find ways to replicate the parts of work that you enjoyed most in your work-optional life. Weiss's research finds that it's common to have an identity while working that's tied to feeling good at your job and that relies in part on recognition for your accomplishments and contributions. Or, as I think of it, you might thrive on receiving gold stars, which can be harder to find outside of work. Rather than accept that fact, make it a mission to find ways in retirement that you can continue to shine and feel valued. In my case, presenting was the thing I felt best at in my job, so I've sought out ways to continue presenting in my post-career life. Because I write and blog about early retirement, it was obvious for me to speak about that subject, but I could just as happily speak to local community groups about ways we can all be better environmental stewards or present about wilderness safety at the local schools. Reflect on what makes you feel good at work, and plan for how you can incorporate that in small doses into your new life.

By crafting a new life in which you're vibrant and healthy, fully engaged intellectually, connected with others around you, and still using some of your best skills, you set yourself up for a long lifetime of happiness and well-being.

FINAL WORK-OPTIONAL LIFE PLANNING CHECKLIST

☐ Complete the "Master Work-Optional Life Questionnaire" in the back of this book to ensure you have thought through each component of your plan, from money mission statement to post-retirement well-being.

☐ Consult the "10 Rules to Live By for a Financially Independent Future" section of this book.

☐ Regularly review your money mission statement, spending, saving sequence, and overall progress.

☐ Enjoy the journey!

CHAPTER 12

Conclusion: Live a Purpose-Filled Life

The purpose of life is to contribute in some way to making things better.

—ROBERT F. KENNEDY

Though I've always been a writer, I never imagined I'd write a book about money. I'm not a financial professional, after all, just a nerd who does her homework and sometimes overthinks things. But I wanted to write this book for the same reason that I started blogging about our journey: because I wanted the conversation about early retirement to be about *life*, not just about money.

Money doesn't exist independent of us, and when we make the conversation about early retirement—as the financial independence, retire early (FIRE) community sometimes does—into one of spreadsheets and optimization and savings rates and "lean FIRE" vs. "fat FIRE," we miss the point. This isn't about amassing wealth for wealth's sake or slapping labels on every choice we make, nor is it about spending the most frugally or hacking the most travel points. This is about living our dreams. Making the very most of our limited time here. Seizing an opportunity that most people through history have never dreamed of.

This is about living lives of purpose, entirely on our own terms.

For most of your life, your identity is decided for you. You're a

237

kid. You're a student. You're a worker in your vocation. Of course, you're also many other things: a son or daughter, a friend, a partner, maybe a parent or grandparent. A person who coaches Little League. A person who throws the best Halloween parties. A person who always sings "Livin' on a Prayer" at karaoke. But the core identity is not always one of our own choosing.

With a work-optional life, however, you have a clean slate to take on the identity and purpose you choose. The psychologist and author Nancy Schlossberg, who has studied retirees in transition, found that the common thread connecting everyone in retirement is the desire to matter.[1] Some of that is about self-esteem, but it also hints at something larger: a desire to contribute beyond oneself, even after leaving a career. Or, in other words, the desire to make a difference. And study after study has shown that those who live lives that feel purposeful are happier than those who simply seek happiness.

In Okinawa, Japan, an island known for the extremely long life spans and happiness of its inhabitants, a concept originated called *ikigai*, which translates roughly to "reason for living," or the idea that you have a purpose in life that gets you out of bed every day. Dan Buettner, author of *Blue Zones: Lessons on Living Longer from the People Who've Lived the Longest*, says that each place known for its extreme longevity has a similar cultural idea, even if they don't have a word for it: having a personal purpose focused on playing a role in your community. Truly living your *ikigai* means being free to engage spontaneously in acts that align to your values, connect you to others, and provide you with a way to feel that your life matters in the grand scheme of things.

Though I'm not a financial expert, something I do know a lot about is mission. I spent most of my career helping cause-driven organizations find theirs, and I hope this book has helped you articulate yours. But think of it as an open question, one you revisit as you grow as a person and as you experience the lightness that comes from achieving financial security. Then, wherever you find yourself in life, don't lose sight of your mission. That mission is what will keep you going when saving feels like a slog, and it's what will make victory taste all the sweeter when you reach your goal.

In this new, work-optional life you're creating for yourself, make it your mission to be a force for good, even if it's in the tiniest ways. Practice generosity, share what you know without expecting anything in return, give back, pay it forward, and be grateful, because if those of us with the most free time and freedom from financial insecurity can't change the world, who can? (Hint: It's us. And we can.)

Imagine a world in which early retirement becomes mainstream. In this world, the average career is shorter, which creates more opportunity for new workers entering the economy. We collectively consume less, easing the strain on the Earth. The average worker can leave the workplace before they hit their 60s, giving them free time at a younger, more energetic age. Living with less work stress and fewer time constraints makes us healthier and more active. Thinking about—and actually acting on—the big questions like the meaning and purpose of one's life becomes the norm.

Consider how many of the big challenges in society we could tackle if we harnessed the energy of everyone living a work-optional life. The early retirement movement is growing rapidly, and the more of us there are, the more powerful we become to change things for the better.

How will you use your power?

Acknowledgments

Before writing a book, I would never have imagined how many people are involved behind the scenes in ways big and small, but I truly have a village of incredible people to thank. Thank you first to the entire Hachette Books team for letting me realize a lifelong dream by bringing this book into the world. I'm still pinching myself.

Of course, without our early retirement, there'd be no book. And without my incredible husband, Mark Bunge, there'd be no early retirement. So thank you, Mark, for being the best financial teammate of all time, as well as a nonstop cheerleader, a thoughtful reader, and a skilled spreadsheet maker. You've taught me how to be generous, given me permission to act on my big dreams, and made me laugh every single day. You're an amazing and inspiring human, the world is lucky to have you in it, and I'm even luckier to get an up-close view.

This book also wouldn't have happened without my marvelous agent, Lucinda Blumenfeld at Lucinda Literary. Lucinda, thank you for believing in me and this project and for your insightful support at every turn. It's a privilege to work with you. Thanks also to Connor Eck and Caitlin Tutterow at Lucinda Literary, who have been an enormous help along the way.

Big thanks to Krishan Trotman, my editor at Hachette Books, who bravely waded out into the murky depths of personal finance with me. Krishan, I'm so grateful for your thought partnership throughout this process, for your incisive suggestions, and for pushing me to make this a book that's not just for math nerds.

Thank you to all the incredible women writers and editors who have been here for me throughout this process. Cait Flanders, your generosity of spirit is inspiring to behold, and I'm so grateful for your friendship and everything you've done to help make this book a reality. Erin Lowry, Kristin Wong, Elizabeth Thames, and Jess d'Arbonne, thank you for sharing your knowledge with me, and making this road a little less rocky. Kara Perez, my podcast co-host and soul sister, thank you for all the cheerleading along the way, and for not yelling at me when I had to put book deadlines ahead of podcast deadlines. Thank you to Michelle Howry, Lisa Westmoreland, and Nora Rawn, who believed in me and in this book. Your confidence has meant so much.

I've drawn so much inspiration over the years from Vicki Robin's foundational book *Your Money or Your Life*, and Vicki, you continue to inspire me. Thanks for being the original financial independence badass, for teaching me to think about money differently, and for continuing to be the conscience of the FIRE community. Thanks to bloggers Pete Adeney (Mr. Money Mustache), Brandon (Mad Fientist), and Karsten Jeske (*Early Retirement Now*) for breaking down the foundational concepts on early retirement that inform so much of the FIRE discussion. Thanks to early retirement godfather J. D. Roth for the invaluable book suggestions. And thanks to Robert and Robin Charlton, who first convinced Mark and me that our math was sound and we could actually retire early. Thanks, too, to all the individuals and families who so generously shared their stories as examples in the book.

I'll forever be grateful to everyone who has read *Our Next Life*, especially those who've commented or emailed to share your experiences. Your support made this book possible, and your stories have informed this book in many ways big and small. Hugs and high fives as well to everyone who listens to *The Fairer Cents*. Stay rad!

It might sound weird in a book about leaving work to thank my long-time employers, but I'm just as proud of the career chapter of my life as I am of achieving financial independence and stepping into the next chapter. For that I must thank the colleagues and managers who encouraged me to be my best self at work and supported me at every step. My heartfelt thanks to Annie Burns, Janet Goss, and Greg Pinelo for being stellar mentors, advocates, and friends, and for showing me that you can be successful at business and still be kind. And shout out to Frances Bresnahan, Oliver Griswold, Kelsey Howe, Amelia Nitz, Megan Sather, Dave Tobey, and Allie Wagner for making the work especially fun and fulfilling (and to Dave for *almost* naming this book). Thanks to Bill Drummond for teaching me all those years ago what it means to be a journalist, and to Ruth Ann Reynen for convincing me that I could be a math nerd *and* a writer. Your words were in my head throughout the writing of this book.

I'm convinced I hit the in-law jackpot when I married Mark, so big thanks to the Bunge family—Ralph, Paula, and Jeff, and Allison Pettersson—for all the love and support over the years, especially when Mark and I told you we were embarking on what must have sounded like a fairly crazy and half-baked life plan. I feel lucky to be a part of the family.

Finally, enormous thanks to my dad, Lewis Hester, who has been an inspiring mentor to me throughout my entire life, as well as an irrepressible cheerleader and my first early retirement role model. You taught me to live with integrity, to fight for what's right, and never to doubt what I'm capable of. I can't imagine who I'd be without you. Having more time to spend with you is one of the most special things about early retirement.

Master Work-Optional Life Questionnaire

Before you make the leap to your new, work-optional life, make sure you know the answer to each of these 11 questions:

1. What is your money mission statement?
2. How will you derive income in the long term without full-time traditional employment? (Check all that apply.)
   - ☐ Market-based investments
   - ☐ Rental real estate
   - ☐ Part-time work
   - ☐ Passive business income
   - ☐ Other:
3. What contingencies do you have in place to deal with unexpected financial hardship? (Check all that apply.)
   - ☐ Low safe withdrawal rate (<3.5%)
   - ☐ Two to three years of expenses in cash
   - ☐ Home you could downsize or sell outright
   - ☐ Extra rental properties you could sell
   - ☐ Home equity line of credit (HELOC)
   - ☐ Funds in Roth IRA
   - ☐ Other:
4. How will you ensure you always get good health care? (Check all that apply.)
   - ☐ Buy ACA exchange plan until eligible for Medicare.

☐ Work part-time to stay on employer coverage.

☐ Receive military health care (Tricare, VA, etc.).

☐ Join health care sharing ministry.

☐ Practice health care tourism for procedures you can plan.

☐ Practice dental tourism.

☐ Other:

5. How will you ensure that you stay physically and mentally healthy? (Check all that apply.)

☐ Set physical activity goals.

☐ Sign up for events to stay accountable.

☐ Sign up for classes or training.

☐ Take on more manual labor at home.

☐ Cook more meals from scratch.

☐ Grow produce at home.

☐ Stay on top of scheduling regular physicals and preventive medical care.

☐ Commit to learning new skills.

☐ Take classes in new subjects or skills periodically.

☐ Stay in tune with new technology.

6. What will be your living situation in each chapter of your life? (Fill in. For example: "Stay where I am, move to a smaller home, move to a new location, travel full-time, RV full-time, etc.")

☐ Accumulation phase:

☐ Early retirement phase:

☐ Traditional retirement phase:

☐ Late in life:

☐ Other:

7. What do you want a typical day in early retirement to look like?

8. How will you ensure that you maintain strong social connections? (Check all that apply.)

   ☐ Focus on making new friends with similar schedules.

   ☐ Make an effort to make younger friends.

   ☐ Make an effort to make older friends.

   ☐ Make more time for family.

   ☐ Sign up for new clubs or community groups.

   ☐ Other:

9. How will you and your partner stay on the same page about both life and money goals? (Check all that apply.)

   ☐ Start your financial planning by thinking about what you each want out of life.

   ☐ Schedule monthly money dates.

   ☐ Allow both partners some spending autonomy (trust plus allowance or fun money funds as needed).

   ☐ Check in often about life goals.

   ☐ Cultivate shared hobbies.

   ☐ Know before you retire what you'll do financially in the event you split up or divorce.

10. How will you define yourself without a traditional career?

11. What is your purpose? In what ways do you want to matter to those around you? What do you want your legacy to be?

10 Rules to Live By for a Financially Independent Future

1. Envision the life you want to live before you assign numbers to it.
2. Invest early and often to create as much magic money as possible.
3. Create systems that help you succeed with minimum willpower required.
4. Constrain your spending while increasing your earnings to supercharge your savings faster than you will by pinching pennies.
5. Remember that everything compounds—investments, earnings, inflation, everything!
6. Prioritize contentment over buying more stuff, which rarely brings lasting happiness.
7. If you're in a couple, include your partner at every stage of planning so it's truly a mutual effort.
8. Always invest in your health.
9. Prioritize close social connections at every stage of life.
10. Strive to live a purpose-filled life, not just a life without work.

Additional Resources

Additional Reading

Your Money or Your Life by Vicki Robin and Joe Dominguez

Your Best Health Care Now by Frank Lalli

What Color Is Your Parachute? For Retirement by John E. Nelson and Richard N. Bolles

Revitalizing Retirement by Nancy K. Schlossberg

Social Security, Medicare, and Government Pensions by Joseph Matthews

IRAs, 401(k)s, and Other Retirement Plans by Twila Slesnick and John C. Suttle

Second-Act Careers by Nancy Collamer

Retire Early with Real Estate by Chad Carson

Can I Retire Yet? How to Make the Biggest Financial Decision of the Rest of Your Life by Darrow Kirkpatrick

The Simple Path to Wealth by J. L. Collins

Online Resources

- *Work Optional* companion site: TheWorkOptionalBook .com—all of the spreadsheets and resources from the book in downloadable, editable form
- *Our Next Life*: ournextlife.com—my blog, with the full chronicle of Mark's and my journey to early retirement, and

in-depth explorations of many of the financial and emotional topics we tackled along the way

- *Early Retirement Now*: earlyretirementnow.com—the best blog out there for those who really want to geek out over early retirement math, especially topics like safe withdrawal rates and sequence of returns risk
- The Crowdsourced FIRE Simulator (cFIREsim): cfiresim .com—a Monte Carlo simulator that's useful for checking your math and assumptions on your roadmap
- Investor.gov compound interest calculator: investor.gov/ additional-resources/free-financial-planning-tools/compound-interest-calculator—especially useful for determining how much to save for traditional retirement. Be sure to use real rates of return to account for inflation and keep things in "today's dollars," not nominal rates that will show future, inflated dollars.
- BankRate savings withdrawal calculator: bankrate.com/ calculators/savings/savings-withdrawal-calculator-tool.aspx —useful for getting a ballpark of how much to save for your semiretired years, because it reflects withdrawals. Be sure to use real rates of return to account for inflation and keep things in "today's dollars," not nominal rates that will show future, inflated dollars.
- IRS information on Rule 72T and substantially equal periodic payments (SEPP): irs.gov/retirement-plans/retirement-plans-faqs-regarding-substantially-equal-periodic-payments
- IRS information on federal estimated quarterly taxes: irs.gov/ businesses/small-businesses-self-employed/estimated-taxes
- CAPE Median index reference: multpl.com/shiller-pe
- BiggerPockets: biggerpockets.com—the most comprehensive real estate education site with in-depth resources

Notes

Introduction

1. Dana Wilkie, "Workplace Burnout at 'Epidemic Proportions,'" Society for Human Resources Management, January 31, 2017. https://www.shrm.org/resourcesandtools/hr-topics/employee-relations/pages/employee-burnout.aspx.
2. ComPsych Corporation, annual wellness report 2012. Referenced at https://www.prnewswire.com/news-releases/compsych-report--employee-stress-and-life-changes-impact-overall-well-being-164262886.html.
3. Lydia Saad, "The '40-Hour' Workweek Is Actually Longer—by Seven Hours," Gallup, August 29, 2014. http://news.gallup.com/poll/175286/hour-workweek-actually-longer-seven-hours.aspx.
4. Dave Gilson, "Overworked America: 12 Charts That Will Make Your Blood Boil," *Mother Jones*, July/August 2011. http://www.motherjones.com/politics/2011/05/speedup-americans-working-harder-charts.
5. Eric Garton, "Employee Burnout Is a Problem with the Company, Not the Person," *Harvard Business Review*, April 6, 2017. https://hbr.org/2017/04/employee-burnout-is-a-problem-with-the-company-not-the-person.
6. Lawrence Mishel, "Vast Majority of Wage Earners Are Working Harder, and Not for Much More," Economic Policy Institute, January 30, 2013. https://www.epi.org/publication/ib348-trends-us-work-hours-wages-1979-2007.
7. Ellen Galinsky et al., "Overwork in America," Families and Work Institute, 2004. http://familiesandwork.org/downloads/OverworkinAmerica.pdf.

Chapter 1: Early Retirement: The Ultimate Life Hack

1. Mark Miller, "Take This Job and Love It," *AARP Magazine*, February/March 2015. https://www.aarp.org/work/working-after-retirement/info-2015/work-over-retirement-happiness.html.
2. Social Security Administration, "Social Security History." https://www.ssa.gov/history/lifeexpect.html.
3. Social Security Administration, "Age 65 Retirement." https://www.ssa.gov/history/age65.html.
4. Dora L. Costa, *The Evolution of Retirement* (Chicago: University of Chicago Press, 1998).

251

5. Bureau of Labor Statistics, "Labor Force Projections to 2012: The Graying of the U.S. Workforce." https://www.bls.gov/opub/mlr/2004/02/art3full.pdf.

6. Rebecca Riffkin, "Average U.S. Retirement Age Rises to 62," Gallup, April 28, 2014. http://news.gallup.com/poll/168707/average-retirement-age-rises.aspx.

7. Rebecca Riffkin, "Americans Settling on Older Retirement Age," Gallup, April 29, 2015. http://news.gallup.com/poll/182939/americans-settling-older -retirement-age.aspx; Art Swift, "Most U.S. Employed Adults Plan to Work Past Retirement Age," Gallup, May 8, 2017. https://news.gallup.com/ poll/210044/employed-adults-plan-work-past-retirement-age.aspx.

8. Robert S. Weiss, *The Experience of Retirement* (Ithaca, NY: ILR Press, 2005).

9. Lydia Saad, "Paying for Medical Crises, Retirement Lead Financial Fears," Gallup, May 3, 2018. http://news.gallup.com/poll/233642/paying-medical -crises-retirement-lead-financial-fears.aspx.

10. Lisa Greenwald, Craig Copeland, and Jack VanDerhi, "The 2017 Retirement Confidence Survey: Many Workers Lack Retirement Confidence and Feel Stressed about Retirement Preparations," Employee Benefit Research Institute, March 21, 2017. https://www.ebri.org/pdf/surveys/rcs/2017/IB.431 .Mar17.RCS17..21Mar17.pdf.

Chapter 3: Create Your Money Mission Statement

1. Dennis Jacobe, "One in Three Americans Prepare a Detailed Household Budget," Gallup, June 3, 2013. http://news.gallup.com/poll/162872/one -three-americans-prepare-detailed-household-budget.aspx.

Chapter 4: Invest to Fund Your Future

1. Jim Norman, "Young Americans Still Wary of Investing in Stocks," Gallup, May 4, 2018. http://news.gallup.com/poll/233699/young-americans-wary -investing-stocks.aspx.

2. Trevor Hunnicutt, "Index Funds to Surpass Active Fund Assets in U.S. by 2024: Moody's," Reuters, February 7, 2017. https://www.reuters.com/article/ us-funds-passive/index-funds-to-surpass-active-fund-assets-in-u-s-by-2024 -moodys-idUSKBN15H1PN.

Chapter 5: Plan Permanently for the Biggest Comforts: Shelter and Health Care

1. "Buying Home More Affordable than Renting in 54 Percent of U.S. Markets," Attom Data Solutions, January 9, 2018. https://www.attomdata.com/ news/affordability/2018-rental-affordability-report.

Chapter 6: The Factors That Dictate How Much You Need to Save

1. Jeff McComas, "Early Retirement," in *The Bogleheads' Guide to Retirement Planning*, ed. Taylor Larimore, Mel Lindauer, Richard A. Ferri, and Laura F. Dogu (Hoboken, NJ: John Wiley and Sons, 2009).
2. Karsten Jeske, "The Ultimate Guide to Safe Withdrawal Rates—Part 1: Introduction," *Early Retirement Now*. https://earlyretirementnow.com/2016/12/07/the-ultimate-guide-to-safe-withdrawal-rates-part-1-intro.
3. Jeremy J. Siegel, *Stocks for the Long Run* (New York: McGraw-Hill Education, 2014).
4. Robert S. Weiss, *The Experience of Retirement* (Ithaca, NY: ILR Press, 2005).

Chapter 7: Your Financial Roadmap to a Work-Optional Life

1. Thomas J. Stanley and William D. Danko, *The Millionaire Next Door: The Surprising Secrets of America's Wealthy* (New York: Simon & Schuster Pocket Books, 1996).

Chapter 8: Accelerate Your Progress

1. Bureau of Labor Statistics, "Occupational Projections and Worker Characteristics, 2016–2026," 2016. https://www.bls.gov/emp/tables/occupational-projections-and-characteristics.htm.

Chapter 10: Make the Big Leap

1. Bureau of Labor Statistics, "Occupational Projections and Worker Characteristics, 2016–2026," 2016. https://www.bls.gov/emp/tables/occupational-projections-and-characteristics.htm.
2. Phyllis Moen, Jungmeen E. Kim, and Heather Hofmeister, "Couples' Work/Retirement Transitions, Gender, and Marital Quality," *Social Psychology Quarterly* 64, no. 1 (2001): 55–71.

Chapter 11: Make Your Well-Being a Top Priority

1. Liz Mineo, "Good Genes Are Nice, but Joy Is Better," *Harvard Gazette*, April 11, 2017. Extensively references the Harvard Study of Adult Development, an 80-year-long longitudinal study that began in 1938.
2. David Ekerdt, "The Busy Ethic: Moral Continuity Between Work and Retirement," *Gerontologist* 26, no. 3 (1986): 239–244.

Chapter 12: Conclusion: Live a Purpose-Filled Life

1. Nancy Schlossberg, *Retire Smart, Retire Happy* (Washington, DC: American Psychological Association, 2003).

Index

About the Author

TANJA HESTER, author of *Work Optional: Retire Early the Non-Penny-Pinching Way*, is a former many things: a former political communications consultant, a former public radio journalist, a former yoga and spinning teacher, a former civil servant, and even a former money novice. Since retiring early from formal employment at the age of 38 along with her husband, Mark Bunge, she devotes all her time to fun and purpose: writing her award-winning financial independence blog *Our Next Life*, podcasting on *The Fairer Cents* and *Adventures in Early Retirement*, volunteering in her community, traveling the world, and skiing, hiking, biking, paddling, and climbing around her home in Lake Tahoe, California. Tanja has researched and explored every aspect of early retirement, from the best strategies for saving to redefining your identity without a career, and applies those lessons every day in her work-optional life, and as host of the Cents Positive retreat for women interested in financial independence. She has a regular column on MarketWatch, she's spoken at Google and at conferences around the US, and she has been featured in the *New York Times*, *Time*, *Money Magazine*, Vice Media, Yahoo! Finance, *Forbes*, Lifehacker, Bloomberg, BuzzFeed, and media outlets around the world.